WHITE ROOTS IN AFRICA

The experiences of a White African

Frederick A. Smith.

WHITE ROOTS IN AFRICA

The experiences of a White African

FREDERICK A. SMITH

JANUS PUBLISHING COMPANY
London, England

First published in Great Britain 1997
by Janus Publishing Company
Edinburgh House, 19 Nassau Street
London W1N 7RE

British Library Cataloguing-in-Publication Data.
A catalogue record for this book is available from the British Library.

ISBN 1 85756 390 5

Cover design Harold King

Photoset by Keyboard Services, Luton
Printed and bound in England by
Antony Rowe Ltd
Chippenham, Wilts

To my wife ELIZABETH
who has supported me so
faithfully both in the good and the bad times
and especially during the long preceding months
I dedicate this short autobiography.

INTRODUCTION

What I record here has been inspired by not only the requests from a number of Kenya-born friends and relations much younger than myself but also a remark heard from the BBC in London suggesting that old colonial settlers record their early experiences, as most of those who arrived or were born there at the beginning of the century have already gone to the 'Great Beyond'.

I am further motivated by the fact that my late father, who went to Kenya in 1910 and who experienced many of the trials and hardships created by the First World War, never made a book of his life. The diaries which he so meticulously kept well into the 1950s were lost during the many moves my parents endured after leaving Kenya. None of his cronies are left and only I have reflections of his many travels covering a large part of equatorial Africa.

May I at the inception of this story of my own life unequivocally state that in writing it I in no manner whatsoever intended to offend the religion, culture or language of any person or group of persons. I was also born free and therefore respect others and their cultures as I expect them to respect mine. Further, I am writing entirely from memory and although the dates reflected may not at times be absolutely correct the incidents recorded are unless otherwise stated faultless.

My story relates to a part of Africa the beauty of which has gone forever and can never be restored: a beauty evolved and created by nature and stretching over time immeasurable, completely destroyed by none other than Homo sapiens. Can any memory of nature be made and retained of anything more beautiful than the soft, silent and calm effect of this privilege which was bestowed upon me by the Great Creator of the Universe and sadly not appreciated until lost?

This is Kenya with its Great Rift Valley lakes, mountains, rivers rain forests, grasslands, beautiful white sand beaches and coral reefs of diverse colours and friendly people of many blends. All children of Africa like me are carved from those beautiful creations of nature referred to above. As a 'White African' I am proud to form part of this grand parade on so selective a part of an infinite and ever changing universe where time cannot in my humble opinion be defined or projected.

In the Kiswahili language, 'N'dio Bwana, Memsahib' – masuri sana – masuri kapisa. (Yes sir, Madam – very beautiful – extremely beautiful.) I plead with all the people on this our unique continent to pray with me for 'Nkosi Sikelela i Afrika'.

CHAPTER I

I was born seventy-eight years ago on Burgundy, my grandfather's farm near Eldoret on the Uasin Gishu plateau a province of Kenya on the equator on the East coast of Africa and at that time a British colony and protectorate. Kenya in relation to this infinite universe is only a small speck on the planet earth, but as described by Mark Twain or some other well-known writer is 'That portion of the universe copied by God when he created the 'Garden of Eden'. I shall expand on the variable beauty of this part of Africa as my story progresses.

My grandfather, John James Dry, was of Irish descent. His forebears emigrated to South Africa where he was born and grew up, and acquired some land in the Zastron district of the southern Orange Free State. He married Miss Magdalene Fouche, the daughter of a wealthy and influential farmer who farmed on Mooifontein also in the Zastron area. This farm is to the best of my knowledge still possessed by the Fouches. He was, from all the evidence I acquired both before and also after I came to South Africa, a most successful and progressive farmer. What motivated his decision to emigrate remains a mystery to me. This decision was only brought to fruition after the Boer War and extensive investigation by him. His final decision and destination must have been resolved over a lengthy and no doubt stressful period. I know he visited Rhodesia and also considered other parts of Africa then opening up and calling for investment and settlers. The risks involving his wife and four children (two sons and two daughters) must also have weighed heavily upon him, not to mention considerable resistance from both sides of the family.

He eventually sailed from Durban in 1910, taking a large consignment of implements, a wagon, horse cart, tools, harness, horses, two-wheeled scotch-carts and a span of oxen with him. He went aboard the British India Steamship *Karapara* to Mombasa in Kenya with its ancient buildings, such as the 16th-century Fort Jesus dominating the harbour entrance, the Arabian dhows, the strange ethnic language and cultures, and the awesome, mysterious ruins of the 13th-century town of Gedi a short way up the coast. It was the port serving the entire East African hinterland. At that time the railway went only as far as Londiani. From there transport was by means of ox wagon to Eldoret which had already attracted some merchants establishing small trading stores, or 'dukas' as they were known, and franchise holders representing equipment and other important necessities to serve the small group of farmers already settling in the area. The small rural town was also often referred to as Sixty-four presumably as it was established on a farm with that number. The settlers came not only from South Africa, but in larger measure from the United Kingdom.

After delays at Mombasa and even longer en route to Nairobi to complete the many procedures involving the movement of his large consignment of goods and also all the red tape to obtain some land to settle on and farm, my grandfather eventually reached Londiani. He told me himself of the many problems confronting him on his way from Londiani to Eldoret which, although only some seventy miles, as far as I can remember was quite a few days' travel by ox wagon in good and dry weather. Unfortunately he arrived there at the onset of what is known in that part of Africa as the long rains.

The roads consisted of ox wagon tracks, traversing swamps and stretches of forest abounding in game of all types. Elephant, rhino and buffalo as well as the big cats were also present in large numbers. Malaria was also prevalent. In fact, all strange and unfamiliar conditions.

He fortunately met a settler here who was involved in the transport business between Londiani and Eldoret. This lightened his burden somewhat, allowing him to pay more attention to keeping his family, bedding and essential foodstuffs reasonably dry and comfortable under the wagon roof, covered by large tarpaulins.

He often spoke of the sleepless nights endured in keeping the lions away from the oxen and also preventing the horses from breaking away and escaping.

CHAPTER II

Where did my first perception of life begin? Difficult to pinpoint, but the first recollection I have of 'being' seems to focus on an incident when I must have been two to two and a half years old. I recall my grandfather's house on the edge of an extremely dense rainforest and being led by him along a small path with enormous trees on either side. It was also at about this time that I heard my grandmother playing the piano and I remember being held by my aunt Julia (mother's sister) and she attempting to teach me to dance.

My real reflection of sound! Yes, also at about this time at night lying on my bed in my grandparents' bedroom when the peace and quiet of an African night on the edge of a rainforest was disturbed and I heard the roar of a leopard and the growling calls of forest 'dassies', the little rodent-like rock rabbits. The pleasant sound of rain on the roof followed by streams of water rushing past the windows are pleasant early sounds remembered.

Also among the numerous delightful recollections are of the horse cart which my grandfather took to Kenya. It was a beautiful two-wheeled black cart with matching fold-back canopy and harnessed by two black horses which fortunately survived the lymphangitis which was well established in East Africa and to which almost all the horses taken there by early settlers succumbed at the time. This cart was kept spotlessly clean and polished and always stored in a shed not far from the house. The harness was neatly hung on the walls of the stables where the saddles were also kept on saddle hangers. The feed cribs were also installed here at a comfortable feeding height. The harness and saddles as well as the copper buckles were polished to a brightness from which you could mirror yourself.

Returning to the roar of the leopard, I later learnt that it was a leopard which was caught in a cage trap not far from the home. This roofed trap was made of logs with a latch door which was held open by a pin stuck to the inside of the cage with a piece of meat on it. Enticed by the meat, the leopard enters the cage and on withdrawing the meat, the door drops and the leopard is captured.

My grandfather was not a hunting type and at no time went on hunting expeditions or unnecessarily killed any wild animals, but this leopard had become so sly and treacherous that instead of hunting for itself, it resorted to entering sheep or calf pens, and not only killing a calf to eat but also savaged and maimed others which then had to be put down. The only time that I know of when my grandfather shot any large animals was when they became a threat to the indigenous or settler inhabitants and the authorities granted permission for them to be shot in order to prevent serious crop damage or injury or death to human life. Refer to Figure 1 which has curiously remained reasonably clear over some seventy-two years and which shows me with my grandfather and the leopard skin on the steps between us. The buffalo head was picked up on the farm and was possibly a victim of the rinderpest epidemic then prevailing in Kenya and which caused very high animal mortality. I also have a rhino foot, shot under the conditions mentioned above – Figure 2 of my grandfather and others.

My grandfather's respect for all living things, including birds and even plants, was so deeply implanted in me that although he made me a catapult, I was not allowed to shoot at birds and it was only used for target shooting at empty tins or a stick stuck in the ground. I have, to this day, retained this high respect for all nature's creations and safaris were never on my agenda. The only exception was when my property, myself or any persons with me were in jeopardy.

My next recollection of pleasurable value was my first Christmas morning when I awoke to find at the foot of my bed a carton wrapped in strange and enticing colours. There was

Figure 1 *Me and my Grandfather.*

also a red mesh stocking-shaped container hanging from the foot of the bed, the contents making interesting bulges. Looking up I saw my mother and grandfather standing at the door, and I immediately wanted to know where these articles came from and what they were.

Figure 2 *Rhino.*

My first surprise was a box from which a small rubber man popped up when the lid was opened. This fascinated me for days. After party blow-out squeakers and other unfamiliar articles were removed and played with, my attention returned to the carton which I carefully unwrapped and from a cardboard box a motorcar appeared. I think it was painted red and very shiny. It had a canopy with two old-type lanterns affixed to the sides near the front doors. No doubt influenced by my family it became my Rolls-Royce and gave me a number of years' enjoyment. When I now often see masses of broken toys lying around in some homes I think back to my childhood days when one toy was cared for and played with for years, and the grief when it was damaged or lost.

At this stage I was living with my grandfather and my mother on his farm because my father was in the British East African Forces throughout the First World War (see picture of my father shortly after joining the army, Figure 3). He was only released sometime after the war and immediately went into training with the Colonial Veterinary Services to enable him to become fully conversant with animal husbandry and the medicines and sciences then available.

Returning to my stay on the farm, I recall that the railway line had arrived and had reached a stage where it joined the farm on the border. A siding was constructed here and named Dry's siding after my grandfather. When I last heard

Figure 3 *Father at outbreak of World War One.*

it was still so named. I also remember there were two engineers involved on this project. They were brothers, very friendly men who often visited my grandfather's home during the period they were there and although I heard their name I could not remember it in later years. Then much later, I pulled into a petrol station in Durban. A car was parked there with the familiar Ermelo registration number and I walked up to the gentleman standing next to it. I introduced myself and he responded, saying that his name was Mardinelli. I immediately recognised a connection with the men who had built the railway line and said I thought I had heard that name as a child in Kenya. To my utter surprise he said he was Bill Mardinelli and he and his brother were the engineers involved with the construction of the railway.

I remember my grandfather telling me one morning that he could not go to the railway construction site where I often accompanied him and where he was employed for a short while as a supervisor. He said he had to go to Eldoret where the bank was. He showed me a piece of paper which he said he would exchange at the bank for some money. I was now a very inquisitive young brat and no doubt thoroughly spoilt. After a lot of nagging he told me that when he again went to the bank he would take me with him.

The day arrived and I was delighted. I was clothed to fit the occasion. My grandfather was in a suit and my grandmother in the fashion of the time, with a hat on which an ostrich feather proudly responded to the breeze. It was fashionable for toddlers to be dressed in naval style uniform suits; I did not take to this white outfit, being continuously restricted and disciplined to avoid getting it dirty.

I sat next to my granddad in his, for those days, comfortable buggy bench cart with grandma on my left. The click-clack sound of the horse hooves on the road and the click-clack on the front harness arrangement again recalls a pleasant memory; hard to believe, it happened about some seventy years ago! We arrived in Eldoret and stopped behind the Central Hotel in a small camped-in area where a nifty stable hand met us. Leaving the cart and horses in what no doubt were his capable hands, we walked off and my grandfather went round to the front verandah, leaving me with my grandmother, which I later heard I always objected to. The purpose for this short delay was to pay some dues to the hotel for attending to the cart and horses. I was of course completely bewildered, this being my first visit to an urban area away from the quiet and vast open spaces on the farm, and all I wanted was the bank. After a short walk my grandfather pointed a finger to what I remember as the most imposing of all the surrounding buildings with an enormous wooden door and large shiny writing on the wall above the door.

This, I was told, was the bank. Thinking back now, what bank was it? Standard Bank of South Africa, Barclays Bank (DC & O), or the National Bank of India? I cannot remember anymore but the Rupee comes to mind, so it was probably the latter. I do remember when I moved to Eldoret with my parents, my father banked with the Standard Bank and a Mr Shaw who had come to the Standard Bank from South Africa boarded with us for a while. We eventually entered the bank and after a short conversation a gentleman behind the counter exchanged the piece of paper (no doubt a cheque) which my grandfather carried, for some coins. From here we went to a shop where I saw some large jars filled with a variety of sweets – peppermints, fruit drops and many others. A friendly Indian gentleman behind the counter handed my grandfather a small square glass jar, containing some sweets in exchange for some of the coins and the sweets were then handed to me. It was a small screw-top jar with a label on its side. Here again my timing might be wrong, but I think it was a Pascal product with that name on the label under the screw top, and above the contents it had a piece of paper explaining that each jar would contain a slip on which one of the letters in the word PASCAL would be on it and once all the letters had been collected, they could be posted to an address in England and a carton containing a variety of very tasty sweets including chocolates would be sent to the collector. Pascal certainly did not court the friendship of parents once this became known to the youngsters. My mother, still a cigarette smoker at that time, received a tin containing some packets of King Stork cigarettes, imported from W.D. and H.O. Wills, Bristol and

London. This information I acquired from a square King Stork tin still in my possession. I often wonder what has happened to these companies?

Other cigarette brands also come to mind such as Flag, as well as other cigarettes and sweets containing picture cards of birds and motor cars which were also ardently collected. Those that still exist today are no doubt very valuable.

It was also at about this time that I became aware of a strange occurrence. By now I always tried to find solutions to any strange phenomena of which I was not previously aware. I was already fully conversant with the habits of various birds, their nests and breeding habits, but now a peculiar breed, not noticed by me before, arrived. These birds started some strange ritual at mud pools near the house and after some performance there each of them would carry what appeared to be a small ball of mud in their beaks, which they attached to a top corner of the house under the roof. This eventually turned into a hollow bowl-shaped structure. Impatience sent me to my grandfather for an answer, where I heard the entire story of migrating swallows in accordance with seasonal climatic changes. This explanation, which my grandfather gave to me with a world map lying on the table, my small mind could not easily accept. How could such a small bird fly over such vast distances and continents with their different landscapes and unpredictable weather patterns? The episode played an enormous part in my cultivating an interest in the many life patterns and disciplines in the total system on Earth with the vast differences in the procreation of life in both plants and animals, in fact in all life, which have evolved on this planet. The different groupings of the same type in various species and the preservation of their territorial rights in accordance with the type to which they belonged became clear to me as I grew older. One of the swallows referred to was ringed by my grandfather before it left and it returned to the same nest the following year.

The time was now approaching for my father to return from active service and for the Smith family to set up home together. I remember the joy echoing from all my relations, but of course more so from my mother, who spent considerable time preparing me for separation from the person who had made such a deep impression on my life, my grandfather – mentor and friend, in whose presence I was secure, afraid of nothing. He was also my teacher from whom I learnt to perceive the wonders of not only this world, but also the heavens. Constellations such as the Milky way and others, as well as the planets Mars, Jupiter and Venus. The heavens became more apparent and interesting as time went on and remain one of my most exciting areas in the entire universe, with the enormous part they played in the various achievements made by scientists in the solar system during my life.

I had by now become familiar with my grandfather's habits and the regular pattern of his daily life. Early to rise and off to farming matters, which always received priority. He would then go to his workshop where he spent long hours at furniture manufacture. This was confined mainly to off-season periods and when circumstances permitted. In those days furniture making was executed manually as electric and motorised equipment was not yet readily available on farms. As he used only hard woods, the exhaustion which it caused must have been extremely high, as also displayed by the perfection in his end product. He made a large variety of household items. Dining-room tables, seating about a dozen people, with the two top chairs fitted with comfortable arms, and other items were completed by him. A fairly large number of these items were brought to South Africa by my parents when they came to settle here permanently from Kenya. These were distributed to distant members of the family after my mother's death, unfortunately in my absence due to circumstances prohibiting my presence when he sold their home in Heidelberg, Transvaal (see Figure 4). I had only a baby chair made for me on the farm at my birth and later used by my children and which I unfortunately lost possession of when it went to my granddaughter now residing somewhere in Pretoria.

Let me now return to my grandfather and his normal routine. As evening approached, he would begin by sweeping his workshop and placing the waste in a gunny bag. The tools were then cleaned, oiled and replaced in their positions in the

Figure 4 *Parents' home in Heidelberg, Transvaal.*

shop. This completed and the workshop locked, he would visit the cattle kraals, calf sheds, sheep pens and horse stables and then discuss matters with his *nyapara* (foreman). In ploughing, planting or harvesting seasons, he would spend almost the whole day in the field, then checking the equipment as they come back in the evening. On arrival in the house, his next stop was the bathroom and finally the sitting-room where at night especially during the rainy season, a log fire would be crackling. This was reading time with light from two safari lanterns, and a Johnny Walker whisky on a small table next to his easy chair. When I first became aware of this, I of course also wanted some. A talk followed on what whisky was and that it was reserved for a 'sundowner' at night, normally restricted to no more than two tots. Grandmother joined us at the fireplace with I think a glass of home-made lemon syrup.

My grandfather's reading was from a very high standard of selected books. He had a large number of shelves packed with a large variety of books. I fortunately salvaged two of these during my mother's life. They are *The Great Controversy Between Christ and Satan* 1895 edition, signed by him and still in excellent condition after a century. The other is the *The Royal Path of Life*. The shelves contained volumes on world history, geography, the stars and science. This confirmed my opinion that he was a most knowledgeable man for those years. He was also kind, always there to listen to problems and to advise where possible, but also exacting and highly disciplined, which he practised, but also expecting too to see the same in those who wished to associate with him.

Some evenings he would suddenly relax, put his book aside and with his eyes fixed to the glowing fire commence singing old Irish songs in a soft and most pleasant voice. There I learnt the words and tunes of 'Irish Eyes', 'Galway Bay' and other old Irish – and English – songs, pleasant and soothing.

A few days before my 'D-day' I was taken to his shed, where I was shown a wooden trap-type cart about the size of an armchair. Inspanned, a white goat, was calmly chewing at some green grass being fed to it. The cart had a seat covered in some soft and comfortable material. It was also fitted with a hinged door which was locked with a latch at the front. After some persuasion, I became more composed and entered it. It was then led away by a young African who had by now become my playmate and with whom many happy days were spent in the shed constructing various models from pieces of off-cut wood and also modelling animals from a black clay only found in certain mud pools on the farm. In Eldoret we lived fairly close to the town and this cart often became my mother's shopping bag. I was very sad to leave my young African friend. It was no doubt with him that I started to learn Kiswahili, the *lingua franca* of Africa and which I eventually mastered to a point where I could speak it phonetically and grammatically correctly and later on pass an oral and written test. I am certain it became the deciding factor in my ultimate appointment to the colonial civil service. It also assisted me to an immeasurable extent in all fields upon which I embarked during my stay in Kenya. In my opinion the ability to converse with any human in a language understood by both parties breeds loyalty and respect for each other.

I found Kiswahili understood at least as far as Lusaka during my various journeys on the continent. The knowledge of this language made me respect the various religions, laws, cultures and customs of the people of Africa.

CHAPTER III

The day I so dreaded arrived and my mother and I moved to Eldoret and the next part of my life began. My cart came with us, the goat to arrive later. Again difficult to fix the time, probably in the early 1920s. We moved into a wood and iron home built on stilts with a corrugated iron roof. My mother began sorting out and arranging her furniture in circumstances which I imagine were also unfamiliar to her in setting up her first home. My father a few days later left for what he told me was his office. This was in the main street of town which later became well known to me. His desk was in a corner of the room which faced a verandah on which the entrance was. In an adjoining room there were shelves on the walls containing bottles and other items unknown to me. On one of the tables was a strange object covered with a cloth. This turned out to be a microscope which absorbed many pleasant hours for me later when my father operated it.

My father was a stranger, virtually unknown to me. A person only seen by me and spoken to on his rare and short visits to the farm during the war was now also fully preoccupied in acquainting himself with his duties and the community. My needs and discipline were left mostly to my mother who believed that the back of a hairbrush was a suitable deterrent at certain times. Dad also contributed his part when time and circumstances allowed, but held opposite views and used an office talk to achieve the necessary. I found this much more effective than the brush which was almost immediately consigned to the forgotten basket.

My parents were well received, no doubt aided in large measure by my father's war record and the award of the Belgian Leopold Cross. I have the medal and certificate in my possession. The medal is still in its original cassette and as far as I can determine the colours of the ribbon are unfaded. A letter congratulating him was received from a friend in Dar es Salaam (see Document A). A party in his honour was arranged at the Country Club shortly after our arrival in Eldoret. Adults enjoyed these parties immensely, but they were despised by children, usually left to sleep on couches, small mattresses or whatever was available.

As time went on I became more accustomed to my father, Lawrence Erasmus Smith, born in the district of Smithfield in the Orange Free State on 31 October 1886 into a family of Scottish descent. He received what education was then available in Zastron where he became friendly with my mother, Maude Dry, also at school there. After he left school he joined his father on their farm but retained his contact with my mother.

The two families became more closely acquainted and the association between my dad and Maude Dry more closely knit. So much so that when my grandfather decided to go north to Kenya, my father had an immediate and genuine reason to accompany them. Over time I heard that he faced utter restraint from his entire family and friends but also struggled to muster sufficient finance for his passage on the *Karapara* and at least enough to feed him on his arrival in Kenya. My mother revealed to me that nobody was aware of this during the voyage and that he somehow managed to avoid any hint of his predicament.

On arrival at Mombasa he immediately began looking for work. Luck was on his side when he spoke to a man who was at the dock to meet someone off the ship. This gentleman gave him a loan of £5 subject to him taking up employment with him on his farm upcountry on arrival there. This my father honoured. Details of this period of his life are not very clear to me except that he started on the farm at a salary of £5 a month and that a month in those days meant every day of that month. This he often remarked on after the introduction of the five-day week.

* * *

Our stay in Eldoret was not for long as my father had to

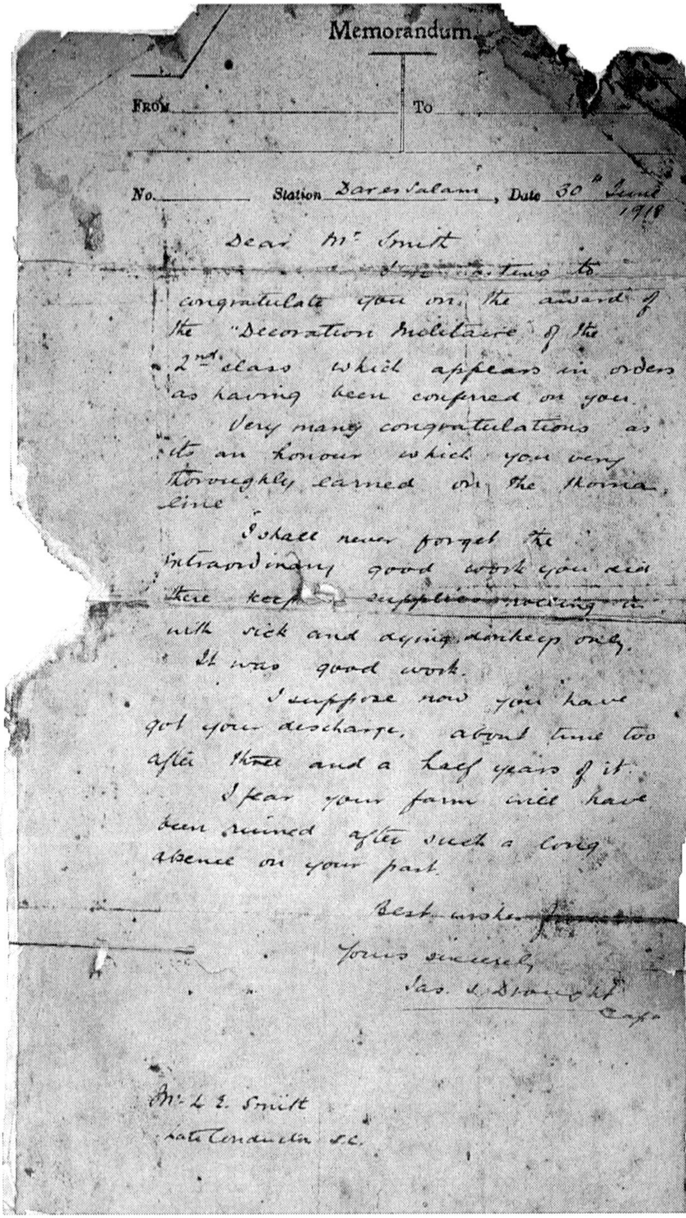

Memorandum

FROM ________ To ________

No. ________ Station Dar es Salaam, Date 30th June 1918

Dear Mr Smith

[illegible] to congratulate you on the award of the "Decoration Militaire" of the 2nd class which appears in orders as having been conferred on you.

Very many congratulations as its an honour which you very thoroughly earned on the [illegible] line

I shall never forget the extraordinary good work you did there keeping supplies moving on with sick and dying donkeys only.

It was good work.

I suppose now you have got your discharge, about time too after three and a half years of it.

I fear your farm will have been ruined after such a long absence on your part.

Best wishes [illegible]

Yours sincerely,

Jas. [illegible]

Capt.

Mr L E Smith

late Conductor S.C.

Document A *Letter from Dar es Salaam.*

Document B *Coat of Arms of Scottish ancestors.*

proceed on his first long leave which Civil Servants were obliged to take every two and a half years and which they were required to take out of the country. This was considered essential in order to counter the harmful effect of living in the tropics to the health of fair-skinned people, an utter fallacy, for the highlands of Kenya with its temperate climate almost devoid of humidity is probably the most man-friendly climate in the world.

This leave privilege included a free first-class passage to any port of the British Empire (excluding tropical areas) for a period of I think six months. We went to South Africa by sea from Mombasa. I don't remember much about this trip, except that I returned to Kenya with a red tricycle, which I later heard had caused many problems aboard ship controlling me from careering all over the deck and avoiding the deck rails which apparently could have landed me overboard.

On arrival back home my father received news that he was transferred to Kitale, some forty-five miles north, to cope with a rinderpest outbreak which had occurred there and which had spread over a large area in the Trans-Nzoia district. It was a serious infection and cattle belonging to both the settlers and the black inhabitants were dying off like flies. This move caused my mother many worries. I later heard that she had accused my father of taking us to the 'white man's grave', a term commonly used about Kitale in those days. Malaria and blackwater fever were endemic and a number of white settlers had already died or lost members of their family from those mosquito-carried diseases. Many farms had also been abandoned. Nevertheless, we went and the move was facilitated by my grandfather with his ox wagons and scotch-carts. He also controlled the entire expedition.

We landed in Kitale in some wattle and daub rondavels with their mud walls, thatched roofs and wood plank doors and windows (see Figure 5). This was certainly not a very entertaining set-up, so much so that I believe my mother wanted to go with my grandfather when he left. However we remained and the first priority was to have the beds assembled and the mosquito nets installed. My mother immediately established a routine that after playing around in the after-

Figure 5 *Our first Kitale home.*

noon I was bathed and put to bed shortly after four o'clock, the mosquito nets tucked into the mattress and tightly secured all around. Here I stayed well into the morning. I was also subjected to the awful experience of having to take half a tablet of quinine every evening, which I apparently began objecting to early in the afternoon. My mother's life was also I believe soured by having to cope with my constant attempts to escape.

Dad immediately became involved with the inoculation programme to curtail the rinderpest epidemic. The vaccine I remember came in wooden boxes or crates from Onderstepoort in South Africa and was contained in brown oblong bottles, neatly packed and protected by straw and sawdust. Peculiarly in those days consignments arrived without any serious losses or damage. The syringes used were large and so constructed that they could contain quite a number of doses, making it possible to facilitate speedy injection of the cattle herded into wooden passages known as cattle crushes leading from a *boma* (kraal) where they were assembled.

My father would walk along injecting each animal. A full syringe was kept ready for him and exchanged without having to stop. He was eventually able to inoculate an unbelievably large number of cattle in half a day, helped after a while by his black assistants or veterinary scouts, as they were known. Some of them were intelligent and keen young men and anxious to advance their knowledge. Here again my father's knowledge of Kiswahili not only reduced the training periods, but also cultivated respect and admiration on both side. I attracted some attention from these scouts, which also advanced my knowledge of Kiswahili. (See photo of father inoculating, Figure 6.)

Time must have by now reached about the third quarter of 1922 and I was rapidly seeing a period of my life disappearing into eternity, pre-school years slowly fading away, but not forgotten.

It was also at this time that my mother became unwell. I did not know what the matter was, but although she never neglected me, I did not receive the intensive attention I had enjoyed in the past. It later turned out that she was expecting my brother, Ebby. She apparently had a difficult time. The

Figure 6 *Father inoculating cattle.*

only doctor available in the vicinity was a Dr Gowan who was friendly and helpful, but not always available. The comings and goings during this period mystified me, until I was called into my mother's bedroom one morning and shown what to me was a completely strange creature. I had not yet seen a new-born human. I was told that this kicking, squawking little bundle was my young brother. The date, 24 February 1923.

The event was celebrated shortly afterwards with quite a party at the Kitale Hotel, which I think was owned by a Mr Kirkwood and was the social centre for this remote area.

Mr Kirkwood was also the publisher of a small weekly newspaper which I think was called the *Kitale Gazette*.

Soon after his birth my brother became ill – I think he contracted malaria. My father's duties in the field then also became more difficult and stressful. Telephones were not readily available, especially from business centres and suburbs to rural areas, and non-existent in the reserves or African areas. Urgent communication was by means of written notes inserted into cleft wooden twigs and secured by winding cotton thread round the top. These were speedily delivered by keen and agile young blacks then known as runners who were well paid and cared for by their employers. My brother's illness and the rinderpest programme also led to my father's long leave being postponed for quite an extended period. I had also now started attending the Kitale School where the Principal was a Mr McKay ably assisted by a very efficient wife in whose class I began my education. This I am certain must have been in 1924. More settlers were arriving and the area was slowly expanding.

Horse carts were also now being rapidly replaced by motor-cars and especially the black Ford Model T or Tin Lizzies as they were generally known. Although they were an improved means of conveyance in urban areas they were often a real test of the owner's endurance in hilly rural areas. The accelerator was connected to a lever below the left of the steering wheel and the spark control on a similar lever on the right. The motion was controlled by three foot pedals mounted on the floor board below the steering and in turn attached to pads on the fly-wheel.

When in constant use in hilly areas, the pad controlling the low gear soon began slipping and the reverse or centre pad had to be used to negotiate hills. This caused frequent and costly replacements.

CHAPTER IV

By now the Kenya Uganda Railways and Harbours line had reached Kitale, running, if I am correct, once a week from Eldoret to Kitale and back. The train was also scheduled to connect with what at that time was known as the mail train to Mombasa. As the third quarter of 1925 approached, the excitement in the family became very significant to me, for my father's next long leave was now due and we were booked to sail to Cape Town. I was of course overwhelmed by the thought that I would travel in this 'chucka-chuck' thing. The local black inhabitants when referring to the steam locomotives called them *ghari ya mhoto* (the fire wagons) and when in motion they said it shouted *Chinja khuku tupa huku* (Kill the chicken throw it there); when said in Kiswahili this corresponded with the sound and rhythm of the locomotives.

After my father had attended to handing over his duties, our furniture packed and stored and our little terrier friend Tiny provided for, we boarded the train. In those days rail coaches were separated with no connection between them. These were only later replaced and connected by corridors. Each of these earlier coaches had toilets and basins installed at the end where the entrance from the platform was and from where a passage facilitated entrance to the compartments. Each coach only consisted of the particular class of travel it represented with the number of the coach in the centre and the compartments alphabetically marked on the outside, with a slot into which a card was inserted with the name of the traveller and the ticket number marked on it. My father was privileged to travel first-class comfortably assisted by Thomas Cook and Sons, a fact that afforded larger and more comfortable compartments and also a high standard of service and attention from train attendants.

My mother prepared some food packed into a large picnic basket. We boarded the train sometime in the late afternoon. It eventually moved and I became aware of the 'clickiti-clack' of the wheels caused by the gaps where the rail sections are joined; a sound I became very fond of and also something which influenced my continued enjoyment of train travel. To me a soothing sound, but as often heard by others as annoying. In those days passenger trains were not very frequent especially to smaller towns from main junction stations and were referred to as Milk Trains. They stopped at many smaller stations and sidings for the embarkation or disembarkation of passengers and goods, an uncomfortable and time-consuming exercise.

At the first stop after leaving Kitale an attendant entered the compartment and after checking our tickets he produced a note book and mother arranged for some bedding. At the next stop a bundle containing sheets, blankets, pillows and much to my surprise mosquito nets arrived. After a disturbed and noisy night caused mainly by a restless young brother, the train which had by now – early morning – speeded along with fewer interruptions from frequent stops, reduced its speed and some houses appeared on both sides of the track. When I woke up the rest of the family were already dressed and tidy which was facilitated by a wash basin in the compartment. I was also tidied as well as circumstances permitted and we steamed into Eldoret station. Here to my utter delight my grandfather was amongst friends to meet us.

At Eldoret we moved into a very much more imposing and very long train, with two much larger locomotives to haul it to Nairobi across the high Ainabkoi and Timbaroa areas which I think was at that time the highest point where any railway in the world crossed the equator. This train was to form part of the mail train from Nairobi to Mombasa, and the compartments were much larger and more comfortable. Drinking water from filters was also available on each of the carriages. This train was not so frequently interrupted, stopping only at larger stations or when passengers had to embark en route to Nairobi or Mombasa.

We left Eldoret in the late afternoon and arrived in Nairobi the following afternoon. Here my father was fully occupied finalising various essential matters such as passports, medical certificates and financial arrangements including traveller's cheques. He was again ably assisted by Thomas Cook. In the meantime our carriage was parked on a siding. Everything was completed in time and the train left Nairobi again in the afternoon and eventually on to the Athi plains where a sight met me that was permanently fixed in my mind: large numbers of zebra galloping away and braying loudly. Impala, Thomson's and Grant's gazelle, warthogs, in fact all the fauna then found in Kenya were present in abundance. My father was giving me a running commentary on all the various animals. This was also where I saw my first rhino, standing under a tree a distance away.

At the first stop the bedding arrived, as pre-arranged by my parents. The beds were made by a most friendly person. I wanted to sleep on one of the top bunks with dad opposite me. My mother and young brother were to occupy the bottom bunks. Between them was a small table which when folded down displayed a very useful mirror above it.

Day slowly faded into darkness and frames containing netting wire and then glass were drawn up and blinds let down on each of the windows next to the bunks. Shortly afterwards the train stopped and after our tickets were examined, trays of food arrived, which was thoroughly enjoyed.

After the trays were removed, my father and I settled down on the top bunks and the rest of the family also moved to their bunks. My father pulled up the blinds and I was happy to at least get some glimpse of what was happening outside. I now became aware of the other various sounds which always contributed to my train travels: the sound of the wheels and sometimes the steam noise of the locomotives as they increased power and speed, the echo of cuttings, the hollow sound of bridges and others. The headlights of the loco and forward carriages were also visible from time to time as they went around bends in the line.

Let me return to this happy holiday with our arrival in

Mombasa, a noisy and strange place to me on that first encounter and overnight stay. Next morning came the great moment when onto the boat we went and were taken to our cabin on one of the decks. It was not very large, but very comfortable. I can still remember to this day that when you woke up in the morning there was a most delightful and tasty apple on the bedside table. While my mum settled down with my brother in the cabin, my father took me on to the deck where a number of noisy cranes were actively loading a variety of articles into the holds with trains shunting in all directions. I was fascinated by everything, including small boats tied to the side of the ship and also the friendly people on board, all dressed in white uniforms.

The name of the vessel, again a British India steamship, was the SS *Karanja*. Not very large as steamers go today, but well equipped for passenger service. There were two dining-rooms and lounges – one first and the other tourist. An excellent band performed at various times during the day and during the evenings when everything in the main lounge was arranged for dancing. Neatly arranged deck chairs afforded many relaxed hours drowsily gazing into nothing but expectations and dreaming of what the journey would offer.

Whilst my father and I were on deck the ship slowly began moving away from the pier where many people had gathered waving bon voyage to relations or friends. We moved further into the harbour, turned round and after some blasts from the siren on the funnel and the sound of water disturbance from the rear we slowly commenced moving out of Kilindini harbour. We were soon completely relaxed and out of sight of land.

We arrived off Zanzibar Island early the following morning and anchored offshore. A number of merchants, neat and friendly, Indian or maybe also Arabs, came aboard and after spreading small mats on the deck, displayed a variety of 'fuji' silk and cotton clothes of all sizes and descriptions. Handmade jewellery – gold and silver most attractively designed – as well as pearl necklaces were also in abundance. The competition between these merchants was intense and when a price was given for an article, it was always done in a whisper.

Zanzibar as far as my knowledge stretches is one of the

oldest inhabited areas South of Mombasa, Arabs in dhows arriving there many centuries ago. What I record here now is no doubt well known, but they are memories of what I saw there more than six decades ago. The development on the island was in my opinion obviously done by the early Arabs who arrived there. The architecture was unique in its own way – narrow streets along all the buildings in the old area – the wood carvings exotic. Beautiful large wooden doors with very attractive patterns of different design on each of them. I often wonder whether these carvings carried an historical message. There was also a miscellaneous collection of other wood carvings, all beautifully done. Trays, spoons and various other objects were displayed on the streets and business again was highly competitive.

Zanzibar made a very deep impression on me, both then and on later visits. I imagine the different cultures and dress styles which were strange to me cultivated my interest. I seemed to perceive a more ancient and constant culture to what I had noticed before then. I trust that this beautiful island will be preserved at least to some extent for posterity.

It was also here that some young African boys about ten to twelve years old appeared next to the ship as if from nowhere. They looked up at us on the deck rails, clapping their hands and pointing to their mouths and any coin thrown into the sea would invariably be retrieved by them and shown before placing it into their mouths. Everybody enjoyed watching these little chaps, who did well out of me. I often wonder thinking back how they managed to survive the sharks when they appear to be so plentiful and dangerous these days.

From Zanzibar we sailed on to Dar es Salaam where we again anchored offshore near the entrance to the harbour which was blocked by a German vessel sunk there during World War One. Dad and I went ashore by way of a small boat. We enjoyed the large variety of flowers and the scenery, as well as the buildings, some of them, as I was told, dating back to the German era. Dar es Salaam was to me one of the most attractive harbours on the east coast of Africa – white beaches and coconut palms everywhere. We were again well received by the inhabitants. After spending some time walking around and being taken on a short taxi journey, we enjoyed some pleasing refreshments at a hotel or restaurant near the main beach. We then returned to the boat.

On a subsequent visit I took photographs of the New Africa Hotel and the entrance to government house with old motor cars and *askaris* (policemen) (see Figures 7 and 8).

Figure 7 *New Africa Hotel, Dar es Salaam.*

Figure 8 *Entrance to Government House, Dar es Salaam.*

I was apparently a very wise and talkative young man when we returned to the *Karanja*. But from here onwards my pleasures were somewhat curtailed, not only by becoming seasick, but also having to baby-sit at night with a hostile young brother while my parents went to dinner and relaxed, chatting to fellow passengers enjoying the music and other activities upstairs.

Our next stop was off Madagascar, but the senses in my young brain only fully returned when we reached Beira. Here I remember becoming aware of the Portuguese culture and building styles for the first time, as also their mode of transport. I was not very impressed with Beira at that time. Our next stop at Lourenço Marques (now Maputo), where we called next, left both bad and very pleasant recollections. I abhorred the prison dungeons used there during the early Portuguese occupation. They were dark and depressing, and I remember begging my father to get us out quickly (see Figure 9). It may well be that only very dangerous criminals and murderers were gaoled here, but they certainly did not appeal to me.

My pleasant memories relate to the Polano Hotel which was already in operation then, and still the stop-over and tourist holiday resort. We enjoyed a good lunch there.

Figure 9 *Dungeon or prison in Lourenco Marques.*

The public transport here was by means of rail car platforms, fitted with benches, accommodating four passengers, without roofs and only large umbrellas for shade. Young men pushed these cars along the rails from, as far as I can remember, the Polano Hotel to the beach and also to the shopping area which offered plenty of beadwork, interwoven baskets, beautifully handmade clothing and many other articles.

On this entire holiday, and without exception, the people were again very friendly aboard ship and wherever we went on land. We could walk anywhere any time, in any part of the continent. Thinking back, I often wonder what has happened to Africa and the world. Why all this violence?

We arrived at Durban and my father and I again went ashore. Here quite a number of new experiences awaited me.

These incidents include an Indian sitting on the pavement in a squatting position with his legs folded in front of him, where there was also a round basket with a cover over it. He was holding a penny whistle in his hand. A number of people had already gathered around him and shortly after we arrived he removed the cover and a large cobra appeared. The man began blowing his whistle, swaying his shoulders from side to side, to which the now aggressive cobra responded in rhythm. I don't know whether it is true, but I later heard that the venom fangs had been extracted from it. This, however, mystified and scared me at that time.

From here we proceeded to the old Beach Hotel on the North Coast by rickshaw. These attractively decorated chariots and their operators were an immediate attraction to me. The decorations were all different in pattern and when carefully analysed all seemed to convey their own story. The headdress and apparel worn by these agile young Zulu operators and their manoeuvres were an early pleasant experience.

The old Beach Hotel was built on stilts with a long plank floor verandah affording a clear view of the beach, in those days spotlessly clean. The entire coastline to the north was also clearly visible, including Umhlanga Rocks and also Durban North. Here my wife and I spent what I consider our most pleasant years in South Africa. This was in a ground floor garden flat in Glenashley Heights, a spacious and beau-

Figure 10 *Inside of Glenashley lounge.*

tifully furbished apartment with a charming view over the sea. It was a well-controlled building with well-mannered occupants, mostly owners. I served on the management committee of this share-block development and was presented with a very attractive silver condiment set when I left which is still in my possession. This was another of my unnecessary and sad moves, one which I regret even more as time moves on (see photo of inside of flat, Figure 10). Returning to our walk in Durban, my dad and I had lunch at the Royal Hotel after which we returned to the boat. The lunch was excellent and the service beyond reproach, a standard retained over the years. During my and my wife's last stay there we always enjoyed their Sunday 'Smorgasbord' lunches.

* * *

I now go back to the last stage of our journey to Cape Town which we reached with short stops at East London and Port Elizabeth, where I did not leave the boat. All I remember of this part of the journey are lights on land from time to time and also the odd vessel passing us in the distance.

Nearing the Cape, we encountered extremely heavy seas. We docked in Cape Town where we disembarked, again assisted by Thomas Cook. We booked in at a very comfortable hotel – was it the Mount Nelson? My mother enjoyed a spending spree at some large shops, Cleghorn & Co and also at Garlicks. She purchased a large variety of articles including gramophone records, not then readily available in Kenya.

In writing this, yet another memory comes to mind which involved mail orders placed with Oxendale & Co in England and despatched to Kenya by sea in large, well-packed parcels. I also recall the frustration caused when being measured for suits and other items of clothing. The only items which caused

Figure 11 *Fouche relatives' car, which took us from Smithfield to Zaston.*

any problems were hats which came in round boxes and were sometimes slightly out of shape.

We arrived in Cape Town somewhere between Christmas and New Year, which gave me the privilege of seeing the Coon-Carnival, or the *Kaapse Klopjes,* with their attractive costumes and music performing down Adderley Street. This is something I always enjoyed on subsequent visits to the Cape and later on television.

From Cape Town we went to Zastron through the Karoo, again a train journey I enjoyed. Our first destination was Smithfield in the Free State where relations of my father were looked up, resulting in long discussions into the early hours of the morning. Here he also met some old school friends, after which we went to Zastron by car. We went to the farm Mooifontein where my grandmother was born. She often spoke of Asvoel Kop, which at that time also lay within the boundaries of this farm (see Figure 11, old cars then in use).

This is also when I became acquainted with the very warm, friendly and interesting Norval family. Mr Archie Norval worked the farm known as Stellenbosch. James his son was at that time touring South Africa with a number of stage artists. James was an excellent pianist, his music was also enjoyed by the rest of the Smith family. I often wonder whether any of the family which included the three sisters, Susan, Drieka and Josephine are still alive (see Figure 12).

When my father's leave was over we returned to Kenya first by train via Nelspruit to Lourenço Marques and then again by boat to Mombasa and finally by train to Eldoret where my father was then posted.

I shall now relate an experience slightly out of date sequence, but I might forget it later on. It must have been somewhere in the period when we were resident in Kitale. I refer to a total eclipse of the sun. My father had warned me about it but I did not know what was going on when it happened. I imagine I must have forgotten about it due to not comprehending it fully. When it happened somewhere about midday the whole world seemed to be going into darkness, until eventually it was absolutely pitch dark. The chickens climbed to wherever they roosted. The dogs barked and the indigenous people

Figure 12 *Three Norval sisters.*

scattered in all directions, shouting in Kiswahili or whatever language group they belonged to that the end of the world had come. What really interested me and what I remember well, was that when light returned to a certain degree, the cocks began crowing. I suppose this is one of the unique experiences not enjoyed by many people during their lifetime. I shall now return to my story in what I hope is time sequence.

CHAPTER V

The time must have by now moved to about the middle of 1926. I had some schooling before proceeding on the previously recorded holiday. This was maintained by my father during the voyage and travels. He had procured some school books, and a time was set aside each day for lessons. This seemed to keep me up-dated and I cannot remember any real difficulties when I returned to school at Eldoret. We moved into a suburb known as Ortleppsville, which had been developed by a Mrs Ortlepp in an area across the Eldoret river and which separated it from the main commercial shopping centre, but within walking distance of each other. The area had been surveyed by her husband (a land surveyor). Dad returned to his previous office in town.

This is also the time that I became more aware of my aunt Julia's husband, Uncle Charles Pohl. The Pohls had also arrived in Kenya before the war and my uncle's family came from the Eastern Cape, accompanied by his father and one of the uncles. His father Harry and Uncle Steyn both settled in the Eldoret area. This Cape family formed part of a progressive and prominent group of farmers and woolbrokers. I think the original woolbrokering concern still exists in Port Elizabeth or East London. Uncle Charles was a highly cultured and friendly person, a real gentleman who later in my life became a friend I shall also never forget. We shared our problems and I helped him wherever possible.

The Pohls had moved to Kenya with a large selection of equipment, horses and other animals. A famous stallion named, I think, Dunn Lawn which they also took with them had in about 1910 taken part in some prominent South African horse race which I am almost certain is today known as the

Durban July. This horse died of lymphangitis fever shortly after they arrived in Kenya.

The 1918 Spanish flu which swept through the world also hit this family very severely. Uncle Charles lost his parents and sister Almine. He progressed well with his farming on a very fertile area north-east of Eldoret. Aunt Julia produced delicious strawberries which she sold in Eldoret where she received popular support. Everything went well with them until like many others in Kenya and in fact over the entire world, he was wrecked by the Depression in the 1930s. In spite of all this he still remained calm and a gentleman in the truest sense of the word. On my first visit to South Africa, after World War II, he accompanied me and we managed to trace some of his long-lost relations. This trip will later be expanded on.

I now return to Eldoret where I left off at the beginning of this chapter and the prosperous but short-lived post-World War I era.

The period was marked by the arrival of the jazz craze which originated in the southern states of the United States of America. It was accompanied by the Charleston, a dance performed to perfection by my aunt to records played on His Master's Voice hand-wound spring gramophones with the distinctive sitting fox terrier proudly displayed on the inside of the lid. Layton and Johnston, Paul Robeson, Bing Crosby and many others were voices and styles most enjoyable to listen to and are still. In different style, Jimmy Rodgers and the Hillbillies also had their place, as also country music and cowboy songs. Bands, too many to remember – Carol Gibbons and the Savoy Hotel Orpheans, Dixieland Band, Victor Sylvester, Mantovani, Joe Loss and many more.

There were some other most interesting people residing in Eldoret. I think of Mickey Eyewaz, an auctioneer who came to Kenya from Turkey, with his much scarred face hinting at past altercations; Daddy Kidson with his match-stick tricks and stories; and Mr Eddy whom I seem to attach to a popular pub and also Tommy Hall who sometimes entered one of the local bars on horseback and caused some daring pranks, providing a beer not only for himself, but also his horse. Oom Koos and Auntie Engelbrecht were a popular and likeable family who owned a large home which they developed into a boarding house catering for young people from adjoining farms, attending school or those working in Eldoret.

This was also the period that I began to acquaint myself fully with ballroom dancing, an exercise I enjoyed all my life until circumstances intervened in the early 1980s. A pleasure later shared and also enjoyed by my wife.

CHAPTER VI

My father, being in the Civil Service, was subjected to many transfers and yet again we had to move, this time to Kitale, where we at least moved into a large and very comfortable house (see Figure 13). Here stabling was available and my father purchased a horse and my equtiation began in earnest (see Figure 14). I attended the new Kitale School (Figure 15). Unfortunately the capture of wild animals for export to zoos all over the world also now began and my father became involved in treating injured and sick animals, a duty I know he lamented (see Figures 16 and 17). I became

Figure 13 *Our Kitale house with Mitford Bowker and cycle.*

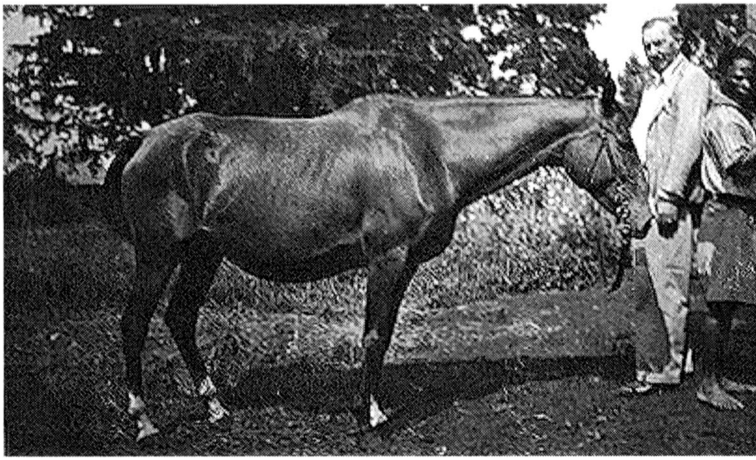

Figure 14 *Our first horse at Kitale.*

very concerned about animals being removed from their natural habitats into captivity – I suppose also prisoners of fate.

My father's long leave was again approaching and this time there were some serious deliberations whether he could afford such a trip at that time. Although passages and train travel

Figure 15 *New Kitale School.*

Figure 16 *Father with injured giraffe.*

were still paid for by the state, certain curtailments such as providing for our future education and also honouring commitments relating to a farm purchased in the Thomsons Falls area of the District then known as Laikipia worried him. After consulting the powers that be he took three months' leave which we spent on the Laikipia farm.

I was pleased to return to Kitale which I already knew. It was situated on the foot of Mount Elgon where there were a large variety of monkeys and indigenous birds which I had also now become aware of. Loeries, parakeets and many more birds of different colours, species and nesting patterns all thrived in the forests on the hang of the mountains.

Kitale was close to the Uganda border, where there was a control point at a hill named Tororo which was known for

Figure 17 *Giraffe being loaded into trucks.*

attracting a high volume of lightning during thunderstorms, apparently because it contained a lot of iron ore. I experienced it one evening when we were staying with friends who lived on a farm near the border, over a weekend (see Figure 18).

Kitale was enjoying the prosperity enjoyed by Kenya at that time. There were some very nice and interesting people living there and the district was expanding rapidly. Good and constant rains and very fertile soil produced above normal yields, mainly maize and to a lesser extent sorghum.

My father acquired a new Rugby Durrandt motor car somewhat resembling a station wagon. Taking what was known as his fourteen days' local annual leave, he decided to take us on a trip through Uganda to the then Belgian Congo.

Figure 18 *Tororo Hill on Kenya/Uganda border.*

We crossed the Uganda border at Tororo and eventually reached Kigoma via Bukoba where he was stationed whilst he was seconded to the Belgian forces during World War I. Here his contingent was involved in a fierce battle with forces from German East Africa (later Tanganyika and now Tanzania) in which he said severe losses were suffered on both sides. The Germans were however defeated and withdrew, and my father was assigned to escort a convoy, mainly pack mules and porters, of captured war material, maize and other foodstuffs to Tanga, just north of Dar es Salaam on the east coast. Considerable difficulty was experienced avoiding the German forces, at that time commanded by a General von Lettow, but he fortunately reached his destination which was also at that time the East African army frontline base. He arrived there suffering from some tropical fever, was granted sick leave and proceeded to Nairobi where much to his surprise he was awarded the medal already mentioned and normally referred to as the Leopold Cross. I remember now that my Uncle Charles Pohl, who was attached to the Bellfield Scouts, a mounted regiment which had also been engaged with von Lettow in the East, which I presume also contributed to my father's convoy reaching Tanga.

The holiday trip was most interesting but a worry to my

parents. Roads were narrow and really only tracks through the grasslands, mountains and rainforests where the now very rare woods such as mahogany and various other types of teaks and hardwood flourished.

We spent the night at a hotel known as the Mountains of the Moon Hotel on the misty peaks of the Ruwenzori Mountain which overlooked the gorilla forests, rivers and lakes not very far away. I clearly remember the interesting calls coming from the forests below the hotel at night. The service at this hotel was 5 star plus and was where my wife's brother also spent his honeymoon. A very popular holiday resort before the Second World War.

This is also where I had my first sight of a pygmy when two little men ran across the road track each carrying a bow and some arrows. We were in an exceptionally dense rainforest area and however much my father tried to entice them out with all kinds of gimmicks, cigarettes, tobacco and bananas, there was no response. Here we also encountered some Watussi. They were very tall men. They had filed teeth sharpened to points which my father said was a custom retained from the time when they were still cannibals. Strangely the Wakamba tribe in Kenya were still doing the same when I left Kenya. These men were considered extremely intelligent and loyal, trustworthy workers.

I am still thankful for all these lovely happy memories which I continued to experience in Uganda, Lake Victoria and the Nile, which we crossed near the Rippon Falls on a newly constructed bridge which had replaced the ferry.

Kampala as far as I remember had already reached city status with a culture of its own. The country was also prosperous producing high quality cotton for export as well as coffee and tobacco and other agricultural products. Bananas of all colours and sizes a-plenty at 50c a bunch – in those days there were 100 Kenya cents to a shilling and twenty shillings to a pound. The city was a beehive of activity with large numbers of well-dressed black men driving black Buicks and what I remember as Marguette sedans. These men were referred to as the Cotton Kings of Uganda. Uganda was at that time governed by I think King Freddy, to conform with the British Mandate then in operation there.

Figure 19 *Lutembe crocodile.*

There were two cathedrals each on its own peaked hill, one Catholic and the other Anglican. At the Anglican cathedral there was an excellent hospital with a Dr Cooke in residence; he was considered the best surgeon in any of the British-controlled East African territories.

We also visited Entebbe where I saw a famous crocodile known by the name Lutembe. It was absolutely tame and appeared after its keeper had spanked a plank on the water for some time on the lake water edge. This crocodile was fed on fish purchased from the keeper by tourists. It was so tame that it allowed tourists to touch it after being fed (see Figure 19). Entebbe on the west shore of Lake Victoria would later attract world attention after a plane carrying some Israelis was hijacked and diverted to Entebbe Airport where they were held by Idi Amin until rescued by the Israeli Air Force coming in at night undetected via Nairobi.

By the time we returned to Kitale I was a well-travelled wise and talkative young man.

As already mentioned Kitale was attracting a large number of farmers and among them was a Mr Mitford Bowker who also came to Kenya from the Eastern Cape in South Africa. He commenced planting pineapples on a very large scale, Queen

Pineapples bearing large and extremely tasty fruit. At this time Harley-Davidson motor cycles also started making their appearance in the colony and Bowker acquired one. They were large and powerful machines. Available to these motor cycles were sidecars, single-wheeled vehicles for one person which could be attached to the left of the motor cycle. This was a comfortable addition with a soft seat, collapsible canopy and a door for easy access. Quite popular and 'swanky' vehicles.

This was Bowker's total means of conveyance, giving him fast and easy access to any area of his large plantations. He was a most likeable person, but full of pranks, perhaps a little naughty at times. We came to know him quite well and he often visited us and we also saw him on the farm (see Figure 13, page 39).

At this time the Turkana people whose tribal area bordered on white-settled areas to the north were involved in not only some ethnic tribal clashes, but also disputes caused by grazing rights, trespassing and damage to fences on the farms bordering this area. This resulted in the impounding of cattle, police border patrols and control. This eventually brought about deterioration between the Turkana and the farmers (see Figure 20). I think these problems were largely exaggerated by the

Figure 20 *Group of Turkana natives.*

usual rumour-mongering that always accompanies incidents of this nature; a fact confirmed by my father's continuation with his regular vaccination programme without, as far as I know, any real problems.

This situation of course afforded Mitford Bowker just the climate for his next obviously pre-planned performance which he put into practice on a very wet Saturday evening. He took his Harley-Davidson, went round to various farmers and told them that he had received an urgent message from the authorities that the Turkana intended invading the white farms during the night and that they were all to proceed to the Kitale Hotel immediately. Amongst these farmers was a Mr MacDonald who had that afternoon collected a new Dover stove which he had imported for his wife from the United Kingdom. He offloaded it still in its white wooden crate under a large tree to the front of his house. In the meantime the moon had risen and as Bowker sped off MacDonald looked out and saw it shining on this crate. With the rain and clouds causing light-variations through the branches of the tree I suppose he imagined it to be a group of Turkana hiding under the tree ready to attack his home. He warned his wife, ran for his double-barrel shotgun and fired at the crate, but failed to observe the result of his action. He was in his pyjamas and dressing gown, but without wasting any more time he took his wife to his old 'jalopy' parked behind his house and left. When he arrived at the hotel, still in his night attire, he was soaking wet, covered in mud and completely exhausted.

A number of farmers had already arrived with more continuing to come in. In the confusion nobody noticed that Bowker was not amongst them.

Nobody, including the local police, knew anything about this threatened invasion. The police immediately began investigating the matter. Bowker arrived at our home sometime during the evening and asked whether he could stay for the night. His excuse was that part of the road to his farm was flooded. No sign of this prank was visible and nothing was revealed by him and everything in our home went on as normal. In the meantime Mitford Bowker was nowhere to be found by the police who also contacted Nairobi with the help of the local stationmaster on his Morse code apparatus, which created more confusion. The time had already moved on to beyond midnight and contacting authorities was not easy to achieve, specially at night. The hotel remained abuzz with further rumours and various stories and information allegedly heard from employees, all third-hand information.

This went on until about 5 a.m. when Bowker left our home for what my parents thought was his farm, but his destination turned out to be the Kitale Hotel where he admitted that he was solely responsible for the incident and that there was no truth in his story. He was charged by the police and convicted on his plea of guilty and fined £25, a heavy fine for those days.

Quite a crowd including farmers affected by this joke had gathered at the court. To Bowker's astonishment the fine had been collected by these farmers but he refused to accept this from the farmers and paid his own fine. He apologised profusely for any inconvenience he had caused and also offered to pay for any real damage suffered by any person for what he now described his stupidity. By now most of the farmers and others involved accepted it as a big joke made by a person liked by everybody. He was a kind-hearted man, always ready to assist where necessary, also enjoying the loyalty and full support from the large number of persons employed on his farm.

CHAPTER VII

Time moved on and the veterinary grapevine brought stories that my father was yet again to be moved.

This materialised shortly afterwards and my father received confirmation that he was to be transferred to Kisii – not very pleasing to me or my parents. I had to move from home into a boarding school at Nakuru with my parents 210 miles away. I now realise it probably helped me to become more independent and eased my entry into high school which had to follow. Kisii was in the Kavirondo district and reserve near the north-eastern shores of Lake Victoria in the Nyanza Province and as far as I recall it was at that time a well-known area for fishing companies. They caught and provided Kenya with what was known as Victoria Tilapia, a pleasant fish with soft flesh and few bones.

My father was well received by the people in the *boma* as these small towns were known. I have some very attractive and well preserved strings of bead work and stools chopped from tree trunks by the Kisii tribe and distinctive to them only.

My primary school days were also now nearing their end and with the Preliminary Cambridge exams ahead I was moved to the new government school at Nakuru (see Figure 21). Although the same curriculum applied, new masters with strange surroundings and youngsters often critical and even rude always affected me to start with. A friendly headmaster, Mr Pratt, soon settled me and I began to earnestly take part in all school sport activities. I played rugby for the school team at left wing, and enjoyed playing against teams of similar age from Eldoret and a nearby private school.

At the annual athletics event, I was fortunate to win some prizes in the long jump and short-distance running. What a

Figure 21 *Nakuru School.*

thrill when I received a Westclox pocket watch for winning the 100 yards! This watch was guarded at all times, spending the nights under my pillow. I also became involved in the Boy Scout movement. Having been a cub at Kitale School I moved up as a Boy Scout, something else from which I learnt a lot and from which I also derived much pleasure. We were selected to attend the Royal Agricultural shows, attending to parked cars and also as general factotums, but in turn enjoyed the delicious pastries which we were allowed to partake of. It was also most interesting and pleasant to watch the animals, implements and new-model motor cars being imported into the country. I think the Ford V8 was seen at the 1932 show for the first time.

I continued to be rather stressed and worried about the imminent Cambridge exams, but they came and went; like all things in life, both pleasant and unpleasant experiences usually contribute some benefits. I got to know and love Nakuru with the school looking down on the lake below with its pink flamingo shores along its entire circumference (see Figure 22).

The school also boasted its own song, but the words are now forgotten except for the last line. It described the school and its surroundings in exact rhythm ending with the words 'A school I shall remember with my love'.My young brother

Figure 22 *Lake Nakuru.*

arrived at the school at the beginning of the year and I was pleased to help him settle in. He had a very successful beginning of his education at Nakuru.

After anxiously awaiting the exam results I was admitted to the New Prince of Wales High School at Kabete near Nairobi. My first few terms there were not very agreeable. The climate was misty and cold and I was a very homesick young man during the first month or two. This continued until I became friendly with the son of an Eldoret farmer, namely Lesley Mousley. We eventually formed a so-called gang which included Colin O'Shea, the son of T. J. O'Shea the Ford franchise holder at Eldoret and also McDermott O'Toole, a cousin of Colin's. I then became more settled and began performing well at sports, with rugby, hockey and athletics my favourite. I played rugby for the school. It was captained by one of our masters, a Mr Larby nicknamed Bull, and also two Gledhill brothers, one nicknamed Ginger. Mr Larby was a Cambridge rugby blue and the Gledhills played for Oxford.

Figure 23 *Prince of Wales School rugby team 1934.*

Mr Larby played as hooker and the Gledhills at scrum half and fly half. I played on the left wing and at times at centre (see Figure 23).

The headmaster was an ex-ship's captain who turned out to be an excellent principal, maintaining a very high standard of discipline and neatness all round. We all respected him and at all times responded to any instructions or requests emanating from his office. Behaviour was strictly controlled and a culture for respect established. Masters and prefects were greeted in a standing position when spoken to.

The head was a Capt. Nicholson and when we had already moved to South Africa in the 1950s there was quite a write-up about him in a number of newspapers including South African lauding him for the solid foundation which he had set at the Prince of Wales as a non-academic person.

A thing I also remember were the school 'trains' which were composed mostly of school boys and girls returning to their homes up-country at the end of each term for the school holidays. These trains were in the care of chaperons and prefects but in spite of them being accommodated in a central carriage I don't think they achieved much in their endeavours.

Figure 24 *Kisumu Pier at Lake Victoria.*

We enjoyed these journeys and it was easy for us to reach the girls' section by leaving our coaches and entering theirs at the first stop. It was night-time and relatively easy to reach the girls undetected and almost impossible for a small control group to prevent this. We chatted and sang all night taking it in turn to keep *cave,* using various whistling sounds to warn of any chaperons or prefects approaching us. Needless to say, more often than not prefects were also involved. When necessary we would hide under the lower bunks behind small suitcases.

On my first journey home I was met by my parents at Kisumu, a port town on the eastern shores of Lake Victoria. Kisumu was the rail export terminal for cotton and other goods exported from Uganda, or as often called, Buganda, as well as from areas of Tanganyika (now Tanzania) which bordered on it. It was also the home port of the holiday cruiser operating on the Lake (see Figure 24). Kisumu also became well known to South Africans during World War II when General Dan Pienaar died in a plane crash shortly after take-off from here. It was also here where the first Imperial

Figure 25 *Imperial Airways Davelin plane.*

Airways Javelin plane landed in 1933 inaugurating the United Kingdom to South Africa passenger air service (see Figure 25).

My hobby at this time was one of my proud successes. I had managed to construct a crystal radio set. This consisted of what was known as a 'cat's whisker' attached to a coil which I manufactured from copper wire removed from an old Ford coil box and which I carefully wound round a hollow cardboard tube with a piece of crystal quartz attached to it. This eventually led onto a pair of earphones. I took the set with me and listened to it at night when I picked up the Nairobi 7LO cable and wireless station nearby at Kabete. I think my father had a Marconi set on which valves or coils had to be changed for different stations or times at night. The changing of these coils did not contribute to very many good quality receptions. It was after 1936 when I returned to Kenya that he acquired a Philips radio set which operated off a 6-volt car battery with excellent reception. I think he purchased this set from Twensche Overseas Trading Co. in Nairobi.

As already reflected in this story I had already became fond of and attracted by good soft music, and Hawaiian music was beginning to make its appearance and such songs as 'Waikiki Beach', 'Song of the Islands', 'Hawaiian Dreams' and others clearly expressed the culture of a kind people and beautiful islands and a picture of the land of its origin to me.

My stay at the Prince of Wales was abruptly ended when I heard that my father was again proceeding on long leave at the end of 1934. I was further shocked to hear that I was to continue my further education at Grey College in Bloemfontein. This decision I could never understand. Leaving a school I had come to appreciate and understand with a culture deeply embedded in me and at a critical stage of my development into young manhood left me distressed and frustrated. I can only think that my father wanted me to get to know South Africa and also the Afrikaans language better.

How well I remember the overwhelming sadness that afflicted me when going to my grandfather's home and having to say goodbye to him. Little did I know, for the last time. He passed away suddenly from cardiac arrest. This was the first of many sad and sudden losses of dear ones that were to be borne by me and my wife over the ensuing years.

CHAPTER VIII

Departure was again from Mombasa which we reached by way of the usual mail train. I remember silently sobbing as we travelled through the Athi plains and leaving all those animals, friends and relations behind.

We sailed on the *Llandovery Castle,* again with comfortable cabins and excellent cuisine. We disembarked at Durban and then went to the Orange Free State for Christmas. I became more aware of the difference in the cultures and habits inculcated by my Kenya schools and the Afrikaans culture then becoming more pronounced and emotional in South Africa. Again this was my perception and I record it without in any way attempting to offend anybody.

I became more calm when I entered Grey College which I

Figure 26 *Grey College School and Buildings.*

was most surprised to find bilingual and headed by a highly respected gentleman in Mr Murray Meiring, a man still remembered, as I heard recently from somebody who also attended the school. I was accommodated in Leith House (Figure 26) and played rugby for the College. I well remember Springbok Park where we played in a curtain raiser for a more important match to follow – probably inter-provincial. I got to know some scholars from the Eastern Cape – Whisky Bayford, the Quicks and others whose names now evade me. I also met some pretty and highly intellectual young ladies, Priscilla Wilcox and Elsa Malherbe whose parents were well known in the Provincial administration and Afrikaans literature. These were friendly and hospitable families who made me feel more settled and accepted, but I still remained homesick.

The fatal use of Anglicisms gave me a struggle in Afrikaans. However, I managed to scrape through, and when I left the housemaster very kindly gave me a silver serviette ring which I still have.

Grey College produced some well-known and important men, who made their mark in various fields later on (see Document C).

Before I relate the following episode I wish to stress that I am not a gambling type and have never been interested in this occupation. My wife and people who know me well are well aware of this. The incident I refer to now was an exception and I can only be grateful that it did not spark off an addiction.

There was an old shoemaker in Bloemfontein who used to visit the College periodically to pick up shoes that needed repair. He arrived on his usual rounds which must have been towards the end of June and after collecting a pair from me he called me aside and said that the Durban July horse race meeting was due shortly and that he heard from a reliable source that a complete outsider, which I seem to remember as Bally James Duff, would win the big race and that it was quoted at 60 to 1. As I had never involved myself in any horse race gambling I could not quite understand this immediately. After he left I somehow became interested and when he returned my shoes I gave him £5 to place on this horse and told him if it won I would share the winnings with him. I had

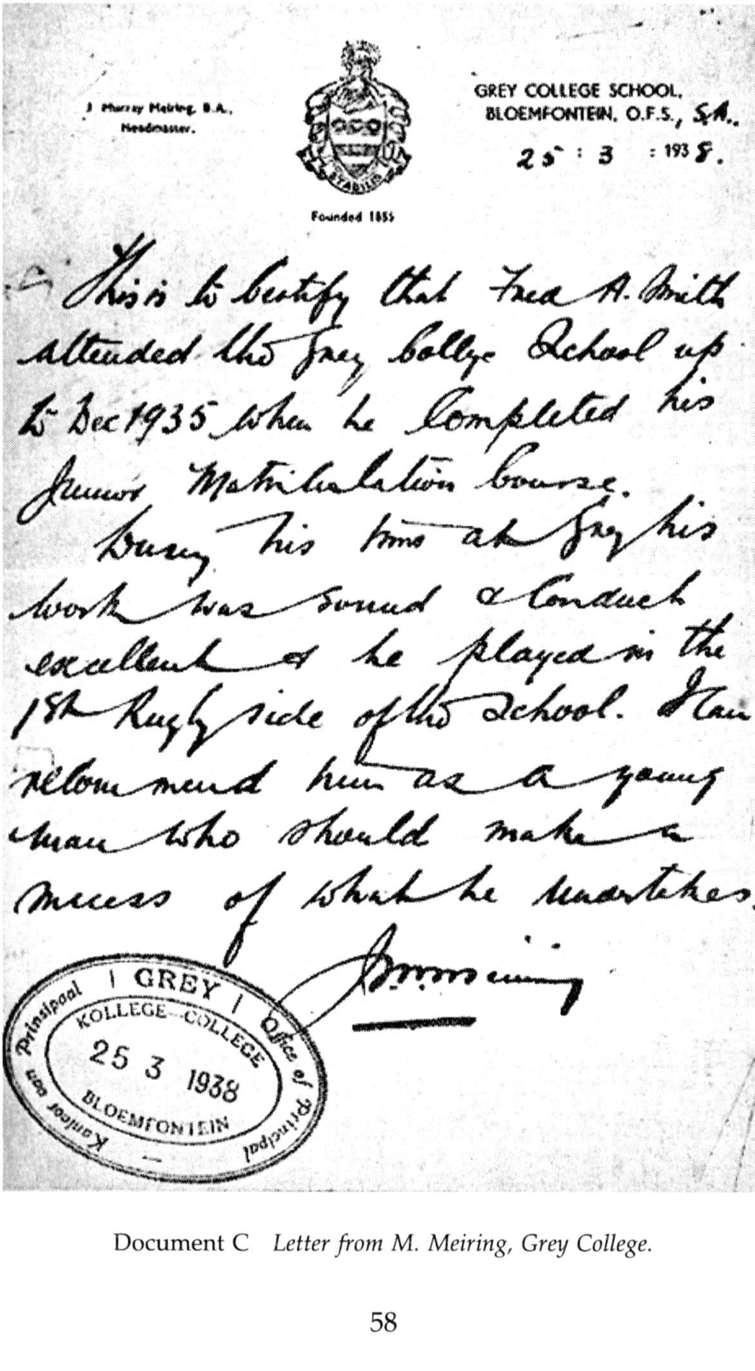
J. Murray Meiring, B.A.,
Headmaster.

GREY COLLEGE SCHOOL,
BLOEMFONTEIN, O.F.S., S.A.

25 : 3 : 1938.

Founded 1855

This is to certify that Fred A. Smith attended the Grey College School up to 5th Dec 1935 when he completed his Junior Matriculation Course.

During his time at Grey his work was sound & conduct excellent & he played in the 1st Rugby side of the School. I can recommend him as a young man who should make a success of what he undertakes.

Kantoor van Prinsipaal | GREY | Office of Principal
KOLLEGE - COLLEGE
25 3 1938
BLOEMFONTEIN

Document C *Letter from M. Meiring, Grey College.*

collected this £5 from the master who controlled our pocket money, and after passing it over I forgot about it and turned my attention to my studies and sport activities. On the Saturday on which the race took place I was involved in a rugby match and remained totally unaware of this race and my bet, until the following Monday afternoon when the shoemaker arrived. He called me aside and handed me a brown envelope which he said contained my winnings. He was very excited and thanked me sincerely for what I had done saying that I was 'Die beste Engelsman wat ek ooit ontmoet het' (The best Englishman I had ever met). After he left I went into the lavatory, removed this thick envelope from my pocket and counted the money which was, I think in £20 notes. It turned out to be an amount I had only previously heard mentioned by adults when they discussed the price of property and motor cars. I can no longer remember the exact amount, but it must have been almost £100. Nothing was said by the shoemaker. Nobody on the staff or amongst the scholars heard about my windfall and I successfully hid my envelope amongst my clothes in my bedroom locker. I was receiving sufficient pocket money to use for the tuck shop and other necessities and for the trip home.

Thinking back, one wonders yet again what has happened to the very high degree of honesty that prevailed in the people with whom I came into contact in those days. This old man knew by avoiding the College for a few months he could have retained all the winnings. I would have had no recourse and would have endured considerable difficulties with the school administration if they became aware of my participation in betting.

The shoemaker enlarged his business and obtained an agency for some well-known brand of shoes. I visited him whenever we were allowed to go to town and before I left I bought a very attractive and comfortable pair of shoes which he let me have at cost price.

My share provided me with a most joyful and luxurious trip home on the *Dunnottar Castle* which happened at the end of the last term (see Figure 27). The people on the boat must have thought that I was connected to royalty or at least to some large and prominent industrial magnate. Nobody would

Figure 27 *Union-Castle Line M.V. Dunnottar Castle.*

believe me when I told them that I was only an ordinary pupil returning home to Kenya from school in South Africa and that I had saved all I had from pocket money and some travelling money sent to me by my father. This was not a very convincing story and also surprised the purser when I handed him the money for safekeeping. His remark was, 'This is enough to buy a new motor car,' or words to that effect. I managed to meet a few very friendly people at the start of the voyage before the story of my imagined wealth became known and it was my pleasure to enjoy their company during the entire voyage.

Due to fatigue resulting from my long train journey to Durban, some hurried shopping there and no doubt also excitement that I was going home, I did not venture out of my cabin after dinner on the first evening and enjoyed a most refreshing sleep at sea, only waking up in the morning when an apple and tea was brought in by a friendly cabin steward.

I bathed, shaved and dressed and went on deck not very long after daylight when I met more fellow passengers and cemented a few friendships which lasted for years, being retained by letter. This also included members of the crew involved with passenger service. I looked forward to the first night and the dancing to music provided by the ship's band. As already mentioned I was very fond of dancing, and had missed it at Grey College except for the occasional school dance. I was dressed for the occasion, fitted out in a dress suit and all that goes with it; all purchased from the winnings when I arrived in Durban before boarding the boat.

Fortunately I was not affected by the stories or the compliments I received, having been brought up in a home by parents who had no chips on their shoulders. Cheap swank was certainly not part of my tuition. I was perhaps also assisted by the fact that my father had always lived within his means and was in reasonably well paid employment which as already described he earned through hard and dedicated work, when and wherever it was demanded of him.

I was later fortunately blessed with a wife who also came from stock that was not affected by wealth or social status. We both mixed with those who inwardly corresponded to what we were taught to respect. Friends were not bought.

Returning to the boat, I danced all night every night as long as the band played. I also became friendly with a Jewish family who were accompanied by a young daughter who was an excellent ballroom dancer and more or less became my dancing partner for the entire voyage. This family also contributed in large measure to my knowledge and respect for all beliefs and cultures. They were on a short tour to Kenya.

When we docked at Lourenço Marques I took the family on a pleasure trip to an attractive spot to the north (see Figure 28). A very pleasant voyage eventually ended at Mombasa where I boarded the usual upcountry train and was met by my parents at Kisumu. My father was still stationed at Kisii but was already packed to move to Rumuruti in the Laikipia District from where he retired to the farm in 1937. I applied for employment in the Colonial Civil Service and was placed on a waiting list for consideration when the Depression finally subsided.

We had two horses and I spent most of my time riding round and exploring the Laikipia plains and its animals. It was during this period that I found an abandoned new-born

Figure 28 *Picnic spot north of Lourenço Marques.*

Figure 29 *Thomson's Gazelle playing with house cat.*

Thomson's Gazelle lamb. I took it home and fed it on a diet prescribed by my father and on which it seemed to thrive, and it became a member of the family, playing around with our cat (Figure 29). As time went on he began leaving the yard to graze on the green grass nearby, but always returned to the house, until he started to go further afield and eventually began approaching other groups of 'Tommies' which sometimes moved to within a few hundred yards of our house; but although he sometimes remained out for the night he still came home without showing any signs of fear for us or the dogs and cat. His stay-away periods become more extended until he eventually did not make his usual appearance. Although I would sadly miss him, this is what we hoped would happen and that he would eventually return to his natural domain. Some time later I rode off and approached a group of these animals and dismounted from my horse. To my utter surprise one of the group, who had moved further away, remained staring at me and suddenly ran forward and came to a halt immediately to my front. He was calm and I became concerned that I might have broken his acceptance of being where he belonged. I eventually rode off towards the group and he followed me, but on reaching a point close to them he stopped and for a reason I could never quite understand, ran off and again joined this group. This was the last time I saw him as I also shortly afterwards left.

I often visited my Uncle Charles who was staying on my late grandfather's farm adjoining ours and which Aunt Julia had inherited. He was an excellent horseman and at about this time became involved in capturing mature cheetahs which he then tamed and sold to Indian Maharajahs who would use them for what was strangely referred to as 'hunting dogs'. As previously stated I was totally opposed to wild animals being captured and taken to the unnatural, and to me cruel, zoos all over the world. Long discussion followed and although I learnt that they would not be kept in closed captivity but treated with great care and kindness by those privileged to have them, I remained sceptical and opposed to this development as I also was with the giraffes and all wild animals taken to zoos.

The cheetah is a timid animal and the method used was to find them on the flat open Laikipia plains and then chase them on horseback. As commonly known they are extremely swift runners, but only for very limited distances, and when exhausted they lie down. A gunny bag was then placed over their head and their feet tied. An old Ford motor car with a specially fitted flat body with a small enclosed cage on it was then brought up and the cheetah placed into this cage and conveyed to the farm. Here they were moved into a large cage covered with netting wire. These cages were erected in an area where they would not be disturbed and in the sole care of my uncle.

These enclosures were well planned, affording sun and shaded areas and also boxed areas for protection from rain and cold weather. At the beginning the animals were shy and sat in a corner of the cage or remained in the boxed area. Meat and water were left at the door and we watched from a distance out of sight of the animal. Nothing happened on the first day and the meat was removed during that evening, leaving only the water at the door. This was consumed during the night. The water bowl was refilled and the meat replaced in the morning. We again remained watching out of sight. Not long after this, the cheetah crept forward slowly and after looking around snatched the meat and returned to a corner of the cage where the meat was devoured, the cheetah grunting almost all the time.

To cut a long story short, my uncle moved nearer to the cage each day until it eventually took the meat from his hands. The next move was for him to go into the cage. The cheetah eventually became tamed, so much so that it took the meat from him and sat next to him being stroked while enjoying the meat. When I visited my uncle later I was overjoyed to find him walking the cheetah quite happily on a leash. It showed no aggression and even took a piece of meat from me, absolutely house tame, later even entering the bedroom and settling comfortably on my aunt's bed, which she vehemently objected to. The animal was regularly bathed in the Mutara river which flowed past the house with the dense Aberdare mountain rainforest extending in patches beyond it towards the mountain higher up. This animal was always well groomed and happy. After I left, she (it turned out to be a female) was sold through some agents acting for an Indian Maharajah at a very handsome price which no doubt assisted my uncle to afford a reasonably good education for his two children, Harry and Beatrice.

With all the travels and experiences enjoyed up to this time

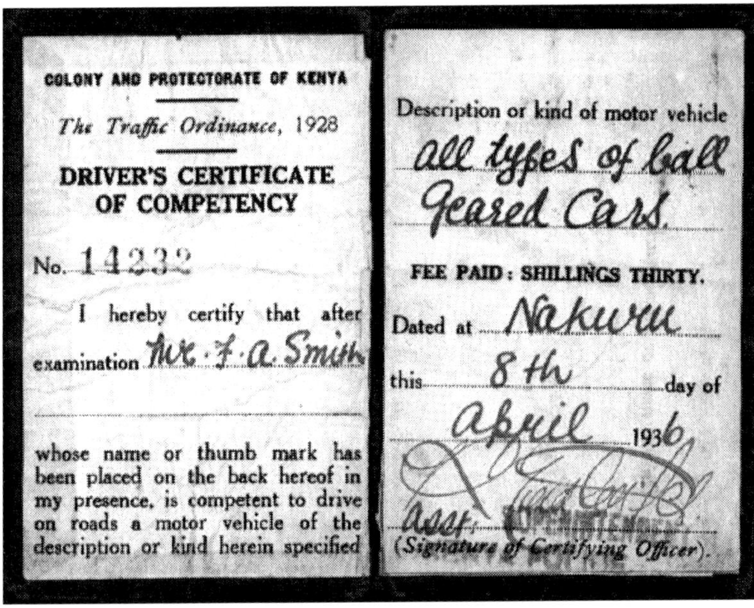
COLONY AND PROTECTORATE OF KENYA

The Traffic Ordinance, 1928

DRIVER'S CERTIFICATE OF COMPETENCY

No. 14232

I hereby certify that after examination Mr. F. A. Smith

whose name or thumb mark has been placed on the back hereof in my presence, is competent to drive on roads a motor vehicle of the description or kind herein specified

Description or kind of motor vehicle all types of ball geared cars.

FEE PAID: SHILLINGS THIRTY.

Dated at Nakuru

this 8th day of April 1936

Asst.

(*Signature of Certifying Officer*).

Document D *Driving licence.*

I now felt rather cut off and lonely at times. What helped me to bridge this period was that I had obtained my driver's licence in 1936 and my father periodically allowed me to use his car to attend sports meetings and get-togethers. This helped me no end (see Document D).

CHAPTER IX

I was now beginning to become bored and agitated and requested a decision on my application for employment in the Colonial Service. A reply was received advising me that I might be offered a position in the Kenya Police when circumstances allowed. This pleased me as I had become interested in police forces all over the Western world, having read and heard of the British bobbies and also Scotland Yard and its important place in society. My father had subscribed to a British magazine covering some famous cases solved by Scotland Yard. I also became friendly with the police officer in charge of the Thompson's Falls Police district with whom I became friendly during his regular periodic visits to the farms in his area, a custom then operating in the Colony. I think he was a Mr Ulyate but again not certain.

It was also at this time that I read about the gangsters in America. John Dillinger and Al Capone were also referred to as rum-runners. This began in America during the contraband period when alcohol was prohibited. Although contravention of this law carried very heavy sentences it enticed people into the highly lucrative illegal trade. I remember the American marine police intercepting large shipments in lonely areas along the American coast at night. Many countries criticized America for this law, expressing opinions that it helped to enhance the crime rate already high there during the Depression which was affecting all countries.

These gangs each had a protection guard very loyal to the gang leader. To my utter amazement I later met a guard of one of these gangs, a Mr Davo Davidson, whose interesting experiences I shall relate later.

In early 1938 I received a letter from the Commissioner of

Police requesting me to report at the Thompson's Falls police station on a certain date, when I would be interviewed. This I did and found the Inspector in charge accompanied by another higher ranking officer. They delved into my history and philosophy and also the history of my father and other members of my family. Everything was recorded. This lasted quite a while. I was then excused and advised that I would again be contacted later. Nothing further happened for a least two months, when I was again advised by post to attend a further meeting at Thompson's Falls. This time the interview was conducted by three officers, all strange to me, and I underwent what I think could correctly be described as intense cross-examination. I was relaxed and revealed whatever I had knowledge of. Fortunately as far as I know I came from an untarnished family with no criminal history. After this meeting we went to a tea break in the private office of the officer in charge of the station. This involved a general chat about all and sundry. Fortunately I was fond of reading and had access daily not only to my father's fairly large library, but also a number of English and American magazines such as the *National Geographic*. I cannot remember any difficulties cropping up. Our travels during my father's employment also of course gave me an enormous advantage. After this meeting I was again told that I would hear from them in due course.

After another fairly long period yet another letter arrived requesting me to attend yet another meeting, this time at Naivasha. Here I faced one of the officers from my previous meeting and two others, including the Superintendent in charge of the Rift Valley Province. This interview again lasted for about two hours during which reference was often made to a file on the table near the Superintendent. After the tea break and on returning to the office I was asked whether I would object to having my fingerprints taken. I had no objection to this performance which also lasted for quite a while during which I was spoken to only in Kiswahili without any difficulty to me as I was by then well acquainted with this language.

After all this I was at least advised that the matter would be expedited and I should receive a decision shortly.

This eventually materialised when I received a telegram advising me that I would be appointed as a Second Grade

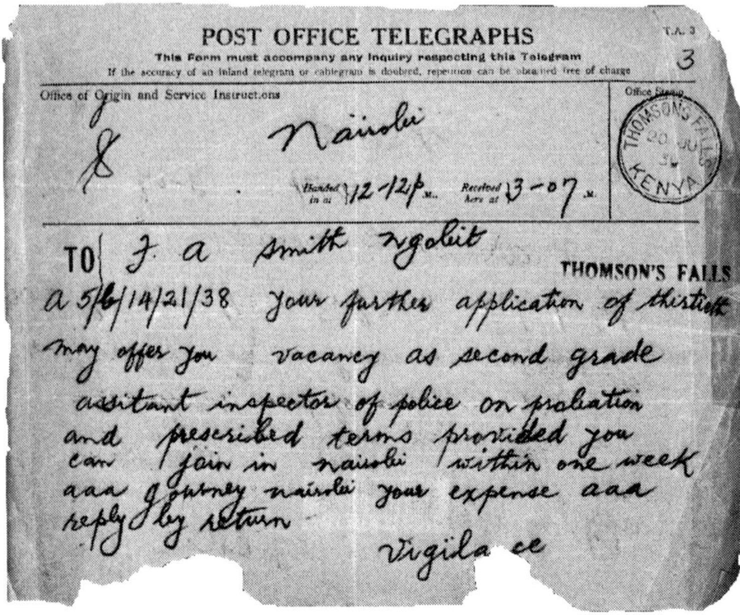
POST OFFICE TELEGRAPHS

This Form must accompany any Inquiry respecting this Telegram

If the accuracy of an Inland telegram or cablegram is doubted, repetition can be obtained free of charge

T.A. 3

3

Office of Origin and Service Instructions

8 Nairobi

Handed in at 12-12 P.M. Received here at 3-07 .M.

Office Stamp: THOMSONS FALLS 20 JU 39 KENYA

TO J. A. Smith Ngobit THOMSON'S FALLS

a 5/6/14/21/38 your further application of thirtieth may offer you vacancy as second grade assistant inspector of police on probation and prescribed terms provided you can join in nairobi within one week aaa journey nairobi your expense aaa reply by return

Vigilance

Document E *Telegram from Nairobi.*

Assistant Inspector in the Kenya Police on three months' probation providing I could report in Nairobi within one week, in other words by 27 June 1939 (see Document E).

While waiting for this final decision I had played rugby at the Rumuruti Country Club and I stayed for the dance in the evening. This was an attractive club under some large old trees on the banks of the Pesi River providing comfortable shaded areas. I was accompanied by Miss Hilda Stewart, a young lady I met on the school trains while still at the Prince of Wales.

A finger supper was provided and while we stood eating a friend of Hilda's walked up to us with a bowl of fruit salad. Hilda introduced her to me as Miss Betty Focks, who then offered me a spoon of her salad which I accepted. She was a beautiful blonde I eventually got to know and married in Nairobi. The greatest gift I ever received, a marriage that has lasted for over fifty-five years.

The time arrived for me to report to the depot in Nairobi. It was situated a short distance from the central city area and across the railway line on the Athi River road. After being taken to my 'digs' I was told to report to the depot commander's office at 2 p.m. I don't think I have ever felt so abandoned in my life.

After dressing myself, shoes shined and generally tidied up, I went to the Superintendent's office. He was a Mr McGowan, a stern-faced ginger-haired officer in a glittering uniform and a whiskered moustache. I stopped at his table and said good afternoon. His reply was, 'Stand to attention. Good afternoon. So you are Smith.' He then read the Riot Act to me in no uncertain manner. Amongst the many rules such as neatness at all times between 6 a.m. and bedtime (except during physical training) officers were to be saluted no matter what the separating distance was. No smoking in public and when in uniform. Caps were to be worn when outside a building or when a salute to a visiting officer was required. Mr McGowan was I am sure a full blooded Irishman, who tolerated no excuse.

From here I was taken to the equipment store where the sergeant in charge was at least friendly and helpful. I was measured for my uniform and issued with a pair of boots, greatcoat, cap, stockings and Sam Browne belt, together with the necessary cleaning materials. After this I returned to my living quarters.

It was here that I met one of the smartest sergeant majors ever. He was a Sergeant Major Ali, highly disciplined, but always readily available for friendly advice when requested. An excellent target shot, too; I once witnessed him achieving possibles at 200 and 400 yards and dropping only one at 600 yards. I was also fond of target shooting which I commenced with at the Prince of Wales school where I failed to win the Leggat Cup in the final shoot-out. This was something I continued to enjoy, later joining the Rumuruti Rifle Club when I eventually joined my father on his farm in the Ol'arabel Valley. I was also able to import a .303 SMLE rifle packed and ball-burnished at Aldershot as well as a P14. Another time much enjoyed by me was when the Kenya Police Orchestra and guard, at the opening of the annual Supreme Court sessions, always staged an excellent performance well attended by a large number of the inhabitants even from surrounding areas.

My training included military drill, physical drill (PT) guard duties and other areas covering protocol. The academic area was covered by various CID and Scotland Yard personnel. I shall not bore you with details of the many fields covered except to mention that in addition we were also taught the intricacies of fingerprints, their lifting and classification. The police regulations as promulgated were also thoroughly attended to, as well as first aid and what goes with it.

We were taken to the Central Police Station for training in all the many procedures: the Occurrence Book (OB), the many registers, taking of statements, opening of investigation files and marking and storing of exhibits, all covered in great detail. Attention to prisoners and their wellbeing and the cleaning of cells were also very important.

At the end of the first training period we wrote a test which I fortunately passed well. After this test I continued to study even over weekends instead of going out when passes were available, which many other trainees took advantage of as most of them had relations in and around the city, which I was not blessed with. However my constant learning and study paid dividends as I was able to pass all the tests that followed.

After leaving the depot I continued studying the Criminal Procedure and Indian Evidence Act as also the coded Felonious and misdemeanour Crimes and local Ordinances.

My active career began at the old Central Police Station near the Norfolk Hotel in Government Road. My first period here was not very comfortable as I was assigned to a week of night duty twice a month. This was most unpleasant as sleep was often disturbed by having to attend court to give evidence on matters arising during the night. Some of the trainees obtained doctors' reports, mainly for insomnia, which exempted them from night duty. I was determined to see this period through so as to complete my training and probation period as soon as possible.

I opened my first bank account when I obtained my salary cheque, an account which I am proud to say has remained unblemished to this day. Part of my monthly salary was transferred to a savings deposit account which I have also kept up.

Shortly after I opened this savings account in Nairobi I was able to buy my first motor car, a Morris Minor Tourer which I paid for in cash and obtained from the agents OMT (Overseas Motor Transport Co.) in Nairobi (see Figure 30).

Before saying farewell to this part of my walk through life, I would like to pay tribute to a few gentlemen who unselfishly and kindly assisted me during my training period. They were Sgt Karioki who was frequently on charge office duty, Sub-Inspector Inderjit-Singh, Sgt Rajah Singh (I hope I remember and spell the names correctly) and also Chief Inspector Ward and Asst Superintendent Swayne and others whose names I can no longer remember and who are probably no longer alive.

It was also at this point in my career when I became fully aware of the heavy responsibility entrusted to me at such a young age. The message carried by my badge symbolized what was expected from me, namely 'Salus Populi' (In the service of the people). The safety and belongings of all persons were vested in my and my colleagues' care and custody. The most frightening thought was always that I should exercise the powers which I carried with extreme care and avoid ever

Figure 30 *Brother and two friends with Morris Minor.*

misusing them. A position which as far as I know I never transgressed.

How well I remember my last night on duty in the charge office when shortly after 8 p.m. the Superintendent in charge of the Nairobi district walked in dressed in a dinner jacket, extended his hand and congratulated me on being appointed to the permanent staff with the rank of Assistant Inspector; I would be moved to the Crime Detection Section with my own office the next day. Why this occurred at night and was carried to me by the Superintendent always remained obscure. I was released shortly afterwards by I think Eric Mullingan who had been transferred from the depot during the previous week. Eric, a New Zealander, became another of my very sincere and lasting friends, a friendship which I enjoyed until circumstances terminated it when I left Kenya for South Africa. On many occasions he advised me to emigrate to New Zealand where his relations would meet and assist me to settle. I have often wondered whether this would have been a wiser option. I am sure the climate would have been kinder to me than the erratic South African summers which I have at times found most uncomfortable. The similarity in language and culture would also have helped us to adapt to the move more easily, but who knows, perhaps not. The grass is always greener across the fence.

My new duties at the Central Police Station initially seemed more relaxed and I began enquiring about the whereabouts of Miss Betty Focks, having heard that she had moved to Nairobi and was working at the Scott Agricultural Laboratories at Kabete and boarding with a Mrs Gethin at Kilimani. The Gethins were old friends of her father and related to Gethin and Hullets who operated a tourist camp at Namanga river near the Kenya and the then Tanganyika border.

Her move to Nairobi was much against her parents' wishes, but as she told me later they became reconciled with the idea because of her loneliness on so large and vast Laikipia Ranch, to which her father had retired from his Thika Coffee farm Kabuku estates, leaving her brother to manage Kabuku.

Her father was at that time a member of the Kenya Legislative Council for the Ukamba constituency which he represented unopposed for many years until he retired and was replaced by Eric Grogan who walked from Cape Town to Cairo to please his future father-in-law who had refused him permission to marry his daughter as he had not yet achieved anything of significance. This walk was successfully accomplished and Grogan married his wife Gertrude. He also wrote a book on his walk, but again I am not sure what he called it, but the name *The Man From the Cape* comes to mind, but this may be totally incorrect.

Eric Grogan went on to become a very prominent and successful farmer developing large areas planted to sisal in both Kenya and Tanganyika, from which a large bag and rope industry materialised. After his wife died, he built and sponsored the management of what he named Getrude's Garden, a children's hospital in Nairobi. He remained a humane and most charming man, contributing to many needy causes in the country.

My wife's father also represented Kenya at the Empire Exhibition in Johannesburg in 1936. We still have a photo of her parents walking in Eloff Street in September with light snow falling (see Figure 31). Other Figures, numbered 32 and 33, also show them in Johannesburg in 1936.

Figure 31 *Snow in Johannesburg in September.*

Figure 32 *My father-in-law in Johannesburg.*

Figure 33 *My mother-in-law in Johannesburg.*

It was also during this exhibition that a motor rally between Nairobi and Johannesburg took place which was won by Fairy Engelbrecht and Fred Hopley in a Hudson Terraplane. This race caused quite a surprise as nobody expected this Kenya pair to make any impression as many well-known drivers in much more sophisticated cars were expected to win the race. I knew both these gentlemen well. Both were from Eldoret. They not only caused a surprise, but also a fright when arriving at their destination they removed a leopard which they had killed in a collision during the night.

I progressed in my studies, only relaxing on rare evenings when my future wife and I went dancing at various night-clubs, Hoppy's in Government Road, Westwood Park and the White Horse Inn, both I think owned by Joan Westbrook. These night-clubs were very well managed and controlled in those days; bad behaviour was not tolerated and the culprits were soon seen off the premises. Admission was also confined to pairs and groups, no single persons were admitted.

Saturday evenings were spent dancing at Torr's Hotel, where excellent dance bands provided the music, Lou Green a name I seem to recall as one of the bands. I enjoyed every moment of those wonderful evenings.

I now became much more aware of the serious crime rate in the Central City area. Shop break-ins at night continued to increase. I decided to camouflage myself as a tramp. With the help of a colleague Allen Peverett, I achieved such a dishevelled image that not even my closest friends could recognise me. On one occasion even my future wife leaving a late cinema show at the Capital Theatre did not know me when I held out my battered hat for a contribution from her and her company, who were also known to me. Visiting back street pubs and walking the streets soon began paying dividends and I managed to penetrate to the very heart of the various syndicates and gangs. This assisted the CID considerably in curtailing these crimes.

CHAPTER X

The war clouds hanging over Europe were beginning to darken and the previously happy and smiling faces began to show signs of sombre reflection and expectation of yet another conflict. Knowing what the First World War did not only to my family but to mankind as a whole, I also became stressed and concerned.

The terror and suffering and torture which Adolf Hitler's Nazi regime had already caused to many independent states in Europe, and his inhumane philosophy of a Herrenvolk, became clearly discernible and the Kenya Police was placed on standby, I think some time at the end of June 1939. This was not only inconvenient and uncomfortable, but also embarrassing at times when you saw your name flashed onto a cinema screen or called out on a loud speaker when at a party in hotels and especially on the odd occasions when Betty and I were on the floor dancing at Torr's in evening dress. I was at that time confined to barracks or to a place where I could be immediately contacted when off duty.

Britain kept her promise to Europe and the declaration of war on Germany was inevitable. The extermination of the millions of Jews by Hitler and his Aryan cult and the horrors that prevailed were difficult to understand by anyone and certainly something which I could not fathom. Why the killing of defenceless women and children, and why so many cowardly heavily armed men obviously finding pleasure in nothing but pure murder?

The total blackout of towns which followed brought a peculiar feeling of distress, and for those of us who had to perform police duties under those circumstances a real trial, although of course nothing compared to the tremendous hardship endured by the defenceless British on that small island against the onslaught of Hitler's Luftwaffe.

My colleagues and I were extremely busy and sleep we only enjoyed when circumstances permitted. I can also remember the sorrow that I and many others experienced when we realised the unavoidable suffering that this insane human also brought to his own people when Britain had to attack the cities where Hitler cunningly concentrated a large part of his armament manufacture.

Some time in 1940 I was transferred to Kilimani, a suburban district bordering on the city centre with quite a substantial variety of inhabitants consisting of wealthy elite whites, both in and around the municipal area, but also extending to smallholdings in the Langata Karen area, with beautiful and gracious homes occupied by millionaires and ex-army officers, who also caused me some unnecessary problems. Sir Delves and Lady Diana Broughton involved in the Earl of Erroll murder saga lived here.

A private club known as the Muthaiga Club and staunchly supported by this group was also in this area. This club featured quite prominently after the Errol murder with all the nonsense that went on there.

A military supply camp was established on some open ground east towards the Ngong Hills with an African village known as Kibera on the south and also fringing on the military camp, containing soldiers from various British territories including a Nyasaland (now Malawi) King's African Rifles contingent. This was a most testing period for me. With blackouts, troop movement, crime on the increase and clashes between indigenous inhabitants, soldiers and unemployed people also contributed to my many problems. Over-indulgence in alcohol, which was available in abundance and brewed illegally in Kibera, was usually the spark in the haystack. This particular brand of liquor was normally referred to as Nubian gin.

I at least enjoyed a comfortable cottage a short distance from the main police station building where I could sometimes relax and charge my batteries for a short time, and appreciate that discipline and dedication constantly to any work assigned to you was the foundation on which any

Figure 34 *My wife and car outside our Kilimani home.*

civilisation could be established and maintained on this planet.

My wife and I had by now become engaged and decided that I should try to obtain a weekend's leave and go to her parents' home in Laikipia to obtain the necessary approval for us to become joined in wedlock: a task my wife had already warned me would not be easy to achieve. Any leave of absence from my duties was also almost impossible to obtain.

I had fortunately by now saved sufficient money to trade in my Morris on a second-hand but very well maintained Ford V8 (see Figure 34). I advised my wife's parents of my intention and awaited a reply confirming the date of our intended visit. As far as I remember a suitable date was set aside during a weekend in October 1940.

I received the necessary permission from the police and awaited this appointment with a certain amount of tension. The weekend arrived and I remember taking the turn-off to their farm after leaving Nanyuki, the town nearest to the ranch. My wife was next to me pointing out various spots familiar to her. As always a positive person. We eventually crossed the bridge over the Washu Nero river which flowed

Figure 35 *My wife's parents' house on ranch.*

through their farm and I saw their home clearly silhouetted on a hill some half a mile away up a slight incline. We were met by some very friendly dogs, which obviously immediately recognised her having accompanied her on many long afternoon walks on the ranch before she moved to Nairobi (Figure 35).

Her father welcomed us and was very pleased to see his daughter. He gave me a firm handshake which made me feel at home and more relaxed, although I was greeted with noticeable apprehension by Mrs Focks. After a most refreshing bath I joined the family in the lounge and Mr Focks invited me to the verandah.

What a privilege to sit on the verandah of a Laikipia home, facing Mount Kenya with its snow-capped peak all the year round (see Figure 36). As the dusk descended and light rapidly turned to darkness the quiet of the evening was disturbed only by the sound of a breeze in the trees and the odd call of a plover. Far removed from the world at war with blackouts, traffic sirens and blaring radios. You look up to a clear sky with myriads of stars varying in size and light to

Figure 36 *Mount Kenya.*

form a galaxy of light and experience a feeling of serenity which I have not yet felt in any other place in all my travels over many years. As the evening proceeds you relax completely until the call of a jackal followed by the laugh of hyenas startles you into alertness.

Our dinner table sparkled with a white linen embroidered tablecloth and cutlery, crystal glassware and serviettes folded to pattern. A setting which would not in anyway fear judgement anywhere in the world. Lighting was provided by a Coleman petrol lamp to which a mantle was attached and which caused problems at times from moths when the shade and screens were not in place.

After dinner we returned to the verandah. After sunset the evenings on the Highlands of Kenya become cooler, especially when breezes come down from the mountain as on this night, when we had to wear cardigans. Low conversation continued after listening to the news from 7LO Nairobi and

Daventry. This was by means of a 6-volt car battery-operated radio.

As talk continued about the future, farming and the suffering of the people of Europe brought about by Hitler and his atrocities and where friends and relations were also involved, it was suddenly realised that the moon was rising, and at that a full moon. Its approach was initially observed from a yellow glow to the right of the high peak of Mount Kenya, slowly raising its ascending rim, playing hide and seek behind moving clouds until shadows of the mountain become more discernible slowly replacing darkness to a full moon, the brightness of which I can only recall on the Highlands of Kenya.

We returned to the lounge where Mrs Focks was waiting for me. She was obviously and understandably worried about how I could provide for her daughter on the meagre income of a junior officer in the Kenya Police; a young lady used to a standard of living well beyond my income at that time. However, after some talk and intervention by her father who was always a most understanding man, the matter was eventually settled and the date was fixed for 21 December 1940, as requested by me.

We returned to Ruiri the following morning. Another difficult hurdle now confronted me as my conditions of service required the Commissioner's permission for marriage. Salary, housing and duty commitments and various other obstacles were involved. These were also eventually resolved and I awaited my marriage with glee. From now on only the most essential expenses were incurred by me and fortunately this was also adhered to by my future wife.

After a one-night honeymoon at the Ruiru Hotel, Nairobi, we moved into my cottage at Kilimani which was fairly close to the police station (see Figure 34, page 79). There wasn't very much available to us in the cottage at that time, although I had a fairly comfortable small lounge suite and we shopped around and managed to acquire an old Philco radio set which was worth its weight in gold, providing music and news.

The New Year period was absolute chaos; serious crime, murders and drunks caused me more than a headache. My wife fortunately remained calm and happy to arrange what

Figure 37 *Our wedding day.*

little there was in the cottage. She returned to her work at Kabete early in January, and for a while that part of our problems were at least settled.

Early in January my parents arrived with my brother Ebby who had passed his Senior Cambridge exams with matriculation exemption and distinctions in all his subjects. He was not only clever, but he also excelled at sports, winning the British Junior Association Boxing trophy and in his last year he was head of school and captained the rugby cricket teams, as well as winning the Victor Ludorum award. My father was also informed that he would be considered for a Rhodes Scholarship after the war, but because of his age, then only sixteen on the February after the final exams, and the idle wait until he reached the age of eighteen or the war ended it was decided to send him to Stellenbosch University in South Africa, where he eventually obtained his BA LL B degree and was later admitted to the British Bar. This part of his story is recorded only as he will feature in my life later.

Violence and crime were still increasing in large measure, contributed to and assisted by the first batch of South African Engineers who arrived. Regrettably they were a most unruly mob, who also caused unnecessary problems. Fortunately those that created the problems were confined to a small gang from their camp initially located at Langata.

On a Saturday evening not long after their arrival they apparently obtained passes to leave camp and went on the rampage in the city centre, the gravity of which exceeded anything previously experienced there. It was later established that the problem started in an up-town restaurant, Chez Gaby, where they ordered some expensive delicacy and then refused to pay. The reason given was that they had come to rescue the British from defeat by the Italians and considered free food a privilege which they deserved. The owner called in the police, but by that time more of these South Africans had arrived from nearby pubs. A colleague of mine who was one of the first police to arrive told me that as they walked into the restaurant the soldiers immediately went berserk and started breaking up everything inside. They smashed chairs and counters and threw one of the tables through the plate glass window onto the pavement, while others looted the shelves.

Some of them tried to calm these few hooligans, but without much success. The police station nearby was alerted and all off-duty officers mobilised, but by the time they arrived almost the entire city was in tumult. Cars were being overturned outside Torr's Hotel and shop windows smashed even in Delamere Avenue. Fortunately most of the police officers had already completed an advanced course in unarmed combat which assisted in averting any serious injuries to them, but which caused some of those who resisted arrest some damage. By the time I arrived the situation was reasonably calm and most of the culprits and the injured taken care of.

The blackout and a contingent of the British RAF also contributed to this type of misbehaviour in Nairobi while they were there. We fortunately had no further serious problems from the Engineers who were confined to barracks and shortly afterwards moved further north.

I wish to pay tribute to the South African Air Force whose behaviour was beyond reproach. The South African Armoured Car Division also gave us no trouble, as also the contingent of women auxiliaries or 'Mossies' as they were well behaved and well controlled.

One must of course in fairness realise that the incident mentioned above was in large measure caused by men alone in a military camp far removed from relations and friends in a strange country, thousands of miles away from home.

I enjoyed some laughs which hopefully were not too embarrassing to those involved. One involved two of these Mossies who came into the police station to report the theft of one of their handbags. While I was recording the complainant's statement – a long process because they had a slight difficulty with the English language – they discussed in Afrikaans their latest experiences and then turned their attention to me and a full dissection of my person. My looks, hair, English accent, eyes, uniform and more were commented on, totally unaware that although my Afrikaans was fairly rusty at that time, I could understand all they said. I found it most difficult to stick strictly to English and keep a straight face. On completion of the statement I gave it to the complainant and in my best Afrikaans asked her to read it and if correct to sign it. I don't think anything could have shocked them more at that moment.

They jumped up screaming and ran out through the entrance to the station. I ran after them, but nothing could stop them. The charge office staff thought they were prisoners escaping, but when I related the story to them a healthy laugh was enjoyed by all.

Although the city centre had generally become calmer, in early 1941 Kilimani worsened. Problems emanating not only from the large influx of various military contingents, but also from what had by now become known as British Remittance men and the Muthaiga Karen crowd.

The Earl of Erroll (Josh) was apparently the ringleader of this particular circle that he associated with at the club and which also contained Diana Broughton. I was well aware of the stories that circulated about this group. Errol had already previously been thrashed, I think at the Nairobi railway station, by a farmer using a 'sjambok', for paying too much attention to his wife. He also owned a farm in the Wanjohi Valley area already known as the Happy Valley, situated at the foot of the Aberdare Mountains near the O'lbaloset swamp, between Gilgil and Thompson's Falls. Some pretty wild parties took place on this farm where Errol had built a large luxurious home. This is an area I got to know very well when I was later transferred to Gilgil.

The following chapter will be devoted entirely to the famous murder which occurred at Kilimani and which involved this crowd and recorded not only with grief but also anger. These idle playboys and girls brought nothing but embarrassment to the bulk of Kenya settlers who developed the colony through hard and dedicated work, and while they were at war defending the very soil this lot contributed nothing but problems. They were also responsible for the uncalled for and unfair phrase, 'Are you married or do you live in Kenya?'

CHAPTER XI

As I am no longer well and riding into my sunset years I shall now record a matter that has concerned me for many years, and on which I think only I have the complete answer.

I realise that more than half a century has gone by and that certain details may have been forgotten by me, but the relevant facts which I have often been asked to relate since my arrival in South Africa, as mentioned in my introduction have been well preserved.

I am also aware of recent radio talks and video recordings, as well as (if correctly interpreted by me) a newspaper report some years ago, which I think appeared in the *Star* that James Fox who wrote the book *White Mischief* found it difficult to confirm certain of the facts as most of those involved were no longer alive.

During the second week of January 1941 Sir Delves Broughton came to the Kilimani police station and reported that he had had a burglary which had occurred through a window leading into his office where he had left a £5 note as a mark in a book which he had been reading and also a revolver which he had cleaned the previous evening before going to bed. The following morning he found the window open and the £5 note and the weapon missing. While I was recording his statement he remarked that he might have inadvertently failed to secure the window latch properly.

After taking the statement and recording the report in the Occurrence Book I left for Broughton's home accompanied by one of my black assistants. On arrival he took me to his office on the second floor where there was a bookshelf on the wall near the window as well as an easy chair on which he said he had left these articles. I looked for fingerprints and any signs of forcible entry but could find nothing.

Outside and next to this window was a down-pipe which came from the gutter on the second floor roof and extended to the ground where a creeper had been planted. Broughton suggested that this down-pipe could have been used to obtain entry through the window. Although the creeper was somewhat disturbed and pieces broken off it, I could not really find anything that really convinced me that any person had climbed this pipe. There was no damage or disturbance to the joint with the gutter and the marks on it were not in my opinion consistent with the marks which would have occurred if anyone had gone up it. I returned upstairs to check whether I had perhaps missed something, but I could again not find anything which altered my opinion. I left the scene entirely unconvinced that any burglary or theft had taken place. On arrival back at Kilimani I phoned Inspector Fentum who was my immediate superior at that time. He came to the station, looked at my report and after a long discussion it was decided to close the case undetected. The remark made on the blue file cover was that although Sir Delves Broughton was a man of high standing, he probably misplaced or forgot these articles somewhere and was now under the impression that they had been stolen. It was also known that he moved around quite frequently, not only visiting the club, but also to somewhere in Laikipia where he went for weekends.

I have recorded this event probably in unnecessary detail, but I have done so because the detail will bear considerable relevance on future happenings.

It was in the early hours of 24 January that the alarming ring on my bedroom telephone which was connected to the police station charge office a short distance from the cottage awakened us. A gentlemen well known to my wife and me, namely Mr Ronny Condon, was on the line from the charge office and reported that there was a black Buick sedan stationary on the edge of a murram (gravel) pit and in the front of the car below the steering wheel was the body of a white person. He was in a kneeling position and on shining his torch on the corpse he observed a mark behind the left ear, which might have been caused by a bullet. He further remarked that the car was very dangerously balanced and also drew my attention to a mark on the road embankment where the car had left the road and that the headlights were on bright and I would have no difficulty in locating it on the Karen Langata road.

Mr Condon owned a small dairy farm at Karen and was on his early morning milk deliveries to various hotels and the hospital. I immediately dressed and after recording the report in the Occurrence Book and instructing the person on duty to advise the CID standby officer I left for the scene accompanied by a constable.

I had no difficulty in locating this scene where the lights of the car were still on bright and found it completely deserted; apparently nobody had arrived there prior to or after Condon's visit. The car carried a Nairobi registration number and was in top gear and I was immediately under the impression that this Buick belonged to Gibbs Auto Tours and was usually parked in their show room in Delamere Avenue where I often looked at it when I was still stationed at the Central Police Station. It was in excellent condition and the first thing that I observed was that the rear seat support straps had both been detached from their positions on the roof between the front and rear seats. They both lay on the floor between the seats.

The corpse was fully dressed in a British Army captain's uniform, but without a cap anywhere in the car. It was in a crouching (kneeling) position with the hands folded over each other about three or four inches below the head which was inclined forward. There was a mark slightly above the left ear lobe. On closer examination I also observed a mark on the forehead which I ascribed to the head hitting the steering wheel when the car left the road and collided with the embankment.

It was obvious that the car was travelling at a very high speed when it hit the embankment after leaving the road. The damage on the embankment and the distance the car still travelled before grazing the edge of the pit to become stationary in such a precarious position supported my assessment of the speed. I paced off this distance and sixty or seventy yards comes to mind.

I returned to the car and examined the interior again with the help of my torch. My attention was now focused on an object protruding from the top corner of the right front door pillar and although it resembled the rear of a spent bullet I could not positively identify it as such.

Among the first police officers to arrive was the police photographer. I am not certain whether it was Arthur Firmin or Dave Simms. He had to wait until the light improved before he could continue. I went on with my investigation and inspection of the area surrounding the scene and noticed that the grass was wet and also fairly long leading from the pit towards the wooded area. I also noticed that a narrow area leading into the grass had been disturbed. I marked the start of this point of disturbance with some stones for further investigation.

The next person to arrive shortly before sunrise was a government medical officer also known to me but his name again eludes me. He was on his way to the Nairobi General Hospital to attend to an early morning operation. He acceded to my request to enter the car and examine the corpse while we supported it to prevent it tumbling into the pit. He cautiously entered the vehicle and after looking at the marks and touching the head he remarked that rigor mortis had already set in.

After leaving the vehicle he stated that it was difficult to reach a definite conclusion, but considering the mark on the forehead and the considerable shock of the car when hitting the embankment, it would appear that death resulted from a broken neck. Stains resembling blood could have been caused by a slight nose bleed.

Other members of the police were also now arriving – I think they were Mr Ulyate from the CID and Mr Langham from the fingerprint section. Mr Langham was then head of that section and had previously been with Scotland Yard. By now the sun was rising and after the photographer had completed his task we lifted the body from the car and when placing it on the embankment we immediately recognised the corpse as that of the Earl of Erroll. He had a gold identity disc on his wrist and amongst other items found in his jacket was a gold swizzle stick and also a letter from a friend posted in Tanganyika enquiring whether Erroll had been successful in arranging a job for him.

Erroll was then Assistant or Director of Manpower. Shortly after removing the body from the car a lady well known in the Wanjohi Muthaiga Club group stopped on the road and came up to the car and in a startling voice exclaimed what I clearly remember as, 'Oh! God he has done it.' She ran off, got into her car and sped away. Although there were so many people involved in this peculiar group, two names come to mind. I would rather not reflect on the name of this lady.

The object in the pillar of the door was removed and identified as a spent small-bore bullet. A similar bullet was found on the floor. I then left the scene for Broughton's home. The corpse and car were still there, awaiting the arrival of the mortuary van and police tow-in truck. When I arrived at Broughton's home I was told that he had left for a safari in Laikipia. I called for the night watch, who was initially very hesitant and obviously afraid of loosing his job, but after a general chat about his family tribe and his job, all in Kiswahili, I gained his confidence and after explaining his rights to him, he told me what he said was a strange experience during the night and early morning.

He said Sir Delves had arrived back at his home that night with a certain lady whose name he did not know and after parking his car, they went into the house and a light came on in a room on the second floor. Shortly afterwards the light was extinguished. Later another car arrived from which a *bwana makuba* (very important man) and Sir Delves Broughton's wife arrived and another light went on. He said this was not a normal occurrence as they usually arrived in pairs or groups and the lights and sometimes music and conversation continued until they again left in pairs or groups, but on this night shortly after the second couple arrived Sir Delves came out of the house and entered the *bwana makuba*'s car by the left rear door and lay down behind the front seat so that his silhouette disappeared. Some time later the *bwana makuba* came out, entered his car and drove off at a very high speed, something Erroll was well known for, often having been stopped at police speed traps.

The night watch went on to further tell me that this whole affair worried him so much that he went to the head house servant and enquired whether he knew what was going on.

He received a negative reply and went on his rounds for the rest of the night. He said another lady came out of the house just before sunrise and entered another car and drove off. Shortly afterwards Sir Delves came walking up the driveway and although his employer did often go for early morning walks he never did so at such a very early time. He said that he also noticed that Sir Delves' clothing and especially his trousers were wet and also that he seemed out of breath and he was breathing heavily. He, however, greeted him and entered the house. I read the statement to him and he affixed his thumb print to it.

Other members of the staff confirmed that the night watch was a regular person, always on duty on time and that they had seen him on duty that night and had discussed the strange happenings with him.

I endeavoured to obtain some idea of the time Erroll left the premises, but could not arrive at an exact time, but from the total information gathered it must have been between 1 a.m. and 2 a.m. I could obtain no further information at the house and returned to the scene of the crime where I had another look around and measured the track made by the car from where it hit the embankment to where it finally stopped with a tape which I had now acquired and as far as I can remember this more or less tallied with the distance which I had paced off earlier in the morning.

I then decided to pace off and time my walk from the scene to Sir Delves Broughton's home. I began at the point where the grass had been flattened and previously marked by me. I followed this disturbed track which led away from the road into a fairly well covered and treed area and out of sight of the road – always on the alert for any definable foot prints. I did this walk in a fairly slow pace and in what I considered was more or less commensurate with the age and physical condition of Broughton. All these facts as also all others involving me in any investigation were recorded in my police note book but unfortunately these books were lost during our many moves in South Africa.

At the trial, which I shall come to later, I was very heavily cross-examined by the counsel defending Broughton. He was a Mr Morris KC from South Africa and who had been briefed by Mr A. J. (Jimmy) Burke KC after consultation with Broughton. This cross-examination went on for a considerable period. He went on harping on my health, age, physical condition and the time taken to do this walk, always returning to the same question over and over again. This went on until he was abruptly stopped by the presiding judge.

I now return to the events of that day. I left the scene after doing this walk and returned to Kilimani Police Station and phoned Mr Ulyate and told him of the statement I had obtained and the walk and also that one of his Karen servants had revealed that Broughton was fond of target shooting which he always did on his Laikipia property. He apparently fixed a target to a tree and then fired at it.

May I record here that I have given an enormous amount of thought to the burglary previously referred to and as far as my memory goes only a £5 note and one revolver were reported stolen when Broughton reported the burglary, but again fifty years is a long time...?

The next I heard was that a Mr Poppy who recently arrived in Kenya from Scotland Yard would continue with the investigation of this murder. This was no doubt a decision taken because of the status of the parties involved and also to have some unbiased and neutral person to continue with the investigation.

This certainly had its advantages, but also some problems which emerged later. By that evening rumours were echoing from all radio stations and before long newspaper reporters were streaming in from all over the world.

Reuters, British and American newspapers were all apparently carrying headline banners, all with their own flavour and tunes.

I also recall that after I withdrew, some bloodstained clothing was recovered from Broughton's garden at Karen.

I think some bullets were also retrieved from a tree on Broughton's Nanyuki farm in the Laikipia area and which local ballistic experts matched with the bullets found in Erroll's car and I think one found in Erroll's head, but other ballistic experts brought in from the United Kingdom or the United States of America disputed this.

As I had been released from any further participation in this case, I applied my time and mind fully to the many tasks and problems that awaited me daily.

I did however hear that the night watch from whom I had taken the statement, retracted it in total and would not respond to any questions when he was later interviewed through an interpreter, by someone who had no knowledge of Kiswahili.

This was as previously mentioned by me, a fatal mistake in my opinion and even more so when the rights are read to an uneducated innocent person. I even found this reaction in

Figure 38 *Thompson's Falls.*

highly educated persons not conversant with legal procedure.

At the trial in which I think Mr Justice Lucy Smith presided and prosecuted by Sir Walter Harragin KC, Broughton was defended by Mr H. Morris KC previously mentioned, the jury returned a verdict of not guilty. The trial judge disagreed with this, stating that the evidence warranted a conviction.

Sir Delves went free and although he said he would return to England, he stayed and Diana retained her old ways and went on as before. Mr Poppy, although a man of very high integrity, knowledge and experience must have found it difficult coming into this investigation. I don't think he had been in Kenya for very long when this murder happened and the language and customs of the indigenous witnesses involved must have been strange to him.

The jury selected from the local residents, if I remember correctly, also baffled me somewhat. Another matter I felt concerned about was that some of the records were not available to James Fox when he wrote his book, if I understood the various reports and references already referred to in this story correctly.

Figure 39 *Barry's Hotel.*

Broughton later returned to England where he committed suicide after more stories involving jewellery frauds began circulating in Kenya and in the UK.

It was at this time that my father started farming in the Ol'arabel Valley, a very fertile area about twenty-five miles west of Thompson's Falls. Here a Mr Gilbert Colvile also owned a farm adjoining ours on the hill above the valley and to my amazement Diana married him shortly after Broughton's death and often accompanied him there.

This marriage also failed and she again married, this time to Lord Delamere (Junior) son of one of the old Kenya settlers.

* * *

Conditions at Kilimani remained much the same. The war was spreading and violence and serious crime escalated, demanding long hours and less sleep. I was fortunate to be granted a few days' leave towards the end of February 1941 and we proceeded to my father-in-law's ranch at Nanyuki.

I stopped in Nanyuki for a rest at one of the well-known hotels before going to the farm. One of these hotels was so planned and built that the equator would cross the bar counter. This was indicated by a white line painted across it. I am no longer sure whether it was the Sportsmans Arms or the Silverbeck Hotel. My wife enjoyed some refreshments and chatted to a friend she met there and I went into the pub where I purchased a shandy in the Northern Hemisphere and took one step to the right and enjoyed it in the Southern Hemisphere. The next chapter will be devoted to this break, enjoyed more than ever before.

CHAPTER XII

We arrived on the farm on Saturday and enjoyed an exciting and relaxing time with some members of the South African Air Force who arrived there in the late afternoon on the invitation of my father-in-law. He often did this to give these young men a break. They did so much to protect our border where we were threatened by Mussolini's forces assisted by the Shifta guerrilla bands which caused considerable difficulties. They took one of our police officers (Mr Carter) stationed at the Moyale border post, hostage while he was walking on the British side of the border on the afternoon before Mussolini entered the war.

Amongst these men was the officer commanding the South African Air Force base at Nanyuki. I think his name was Blackie Swartz. Dinner arrived and they joined us at the table where I immediately noticed that they were highly amused about something they obviously did not want to reveal to us.

Shortly afterwards the news came on from the BBC. When it was reported that a mysterious bomb had been dropped on an Italian base earlier in the day. I cannot clearly remember the name any more but Wajir comes to mind. This report went on to say that the bomb was not that of a type in use at the time and completely strange and from the information coming in from enemy signals it had apparently caused considerable damage. The British military command also appeared to have no knowledge of such an air strike on that day.

Blackie Swartz could no longer contain himself and the whole story came out. What they did was to take an old forty-four gallon petrol drum and load it onto an old plane which was used to carry the mail from Nanyuki to the forces on the border. They packed this drum with whatever they could find and then inserted a fuse into it and took off on the pretence that they were on a mail delivery mission. When they arrived over the target they lit the fuse and then discovered that the drum was very heavy and difficult to unload through the door, which was not very large. During their struggle the light aircraft was also reacting to the load shifted to the door, and they began panicking which further restricted them somewhat. However, they eventually managed to achieve their objective and the bomb was dropped on target. They noticed quite a large explosion as they circled and returned to base safely with the fuel now almost exhausted. After landing they booked off immediately for the Saturday evening, left the base and came to the ranch.

The South African Air Wing, apart from a little fox terrier dog named Pompie who flew everywhere with them and became well known all over Kenya, also had a lion cub which they named Bomber which also often accompanied them.

Although these chaps were a spritely lot, they were dedicated to their task and contributed in no small measure to the ultimate defeat of Italy in Africa and later the Nazis.

The conversation went on, relating some of their stories and how they longed to return home and again join their families and friends. They later came up with another occurrence which was later confirmed by the media and which could have caused problems stretching beyond what anyone could at that time imagine.

It concerned General (later Field Marshal) Smuts who had flown to the base on a visit. The pilot had approached the base from the wrong direction; I cannot remember whether he should have come in clockwise or anti-clockwise, but in any case it was incorrect. Fortunately, minutes before drastic action was taken, the matter was sorted out and Smuts landed unscathed.

I also remember Betty and I discussing a famous old tree with them – it was known as Lone Tree and was just outside Nairobi, about three miles away on the plains. It was an enormous wild fig tree, standing alone with no other sizeable trees near it. Nairobi youngsters used to go out there in groups which we also often joined. There we spread out our rugs and enjoyed playing records from HMV (His Master's Voice) wind-up portable gramophones.

There were also a number of wild animals out there, some quite vicious, but being in a group and leaving our cars parked in a circle round the group with the parking lights on, we had little trouble except on one evening when an old hyena came through. When we saw it, it was alarmingly standing not very far from my wife's feet, but luckily hyenas are dangerous only in packs and true to form this one ran off when we shouted at it. When we enquired about the old tree after leaving Kenya we were told it no longer existed, but we could never find out what had happened to it. It was a great pity because it must have been there for many many years, perhaps centuries, as even the oldest settlers in and around Nairobi were aware of it.

We returned to Nairobi the following day and shortly afterwards I received notice that I would be transferred to Parklands, where some sad experiences yet again awaited me, although it made my wife's life easier as she acquired a lift, daily, from a gentleman who also worked at the Scott Laboratories at Kabete.

He was an extremely friendly man, well educated and helpful. I often spoke to him, a Mr Naismith-Jones, when he dropped off my wife at the police station, and got to know him well.

We also enjoyed the comfort of a well-designed home and established garden (Figure 40). I had by now become afraid of the ring of any telephone, especially at night. It was a quiet area and at least more restful for me.

Our neighbours were professional men. I think an Indian doctor on the one side and a black lawyer across the road, quiet and friendly people. In addition the police staff were more efficient and well disciplined and after a week or two I was completely restored, both physically and mentally. Fortunately man is oblivious of the future.

It was on a Friday afternoon when Mr Jones dropped my wife and as often happened I walked up to his car and spoke to him. He greeted me as usual and we spoke normally about various usual topics. Before driving off he told me that he was looking forward to a visit which he planned for the weekend,

Figure 40 *Parklands home.*

to a friend in the district. I saw no signs of him being nervous or aggravated or in any way different to his normal behaviour. A quiet weekend ensued until about 5 a.m. on the Monday morning when my phone rang and a neighbour of the Joneses phoned me and hysterically told me that he or she (I cannot remember whether it was a lady or a man) had heard two gunshot sounds in close succession and ran to the Joneses home where they saw Mrs Jones in bed and him on the floor between the beds.

I rushed to the scene and as I walked in I noticed a letter on the dressing-table addressed to me personally. Mrs Jones was lying on her back on the bed and Mr Jones on the floor between the beds. They were both still breathing, but I held very little hope for survival. I immediately contacted the nearest doctor, hospital ambulance and my senior officer on night standby. About an inch from Mr Jones's hand there was a handgun. This situation shocked me tremendously in spite of all the serious conditions which had already confronted me in the past and to which my helplessness always contributed but more so involving somebody I knew so well. Mr Jones was gurgling but his wife lay quietly with hardly any sound except a slow breath.

The ambulance and medical aid arrived promptly and after lifting Mr Jones onto the stretcher, we turned to Mrs Jones and as I lifted her onto the other stretcher she opened her eyes widely and gave her last breath.

The letter was clearly written with no apparent sign of the condition in which Mr Jones must have been at the time. He said that he had confirmed a suspicion which he had been aware of that his wife was having an affair with an army officer where she was employed and although he had attempted to rectify this situation it continued and he was going to take both their lives. His letter also contained instructions concerning the distribution of his assets, but which I can no longer remember. They were childless. My investigation revealed that this couple enjoyed a very happy party with some friends on the Saturday evening and everyone expressed how happy and relaxed Mr Jones appeared to be. The weapon used he had borrowed on some pretence or other from a friend.

This incident traumatised me, but in more serious manner my wife who worked with him for a long time and also enjoyed lifts in his car.

When I later reflected on the Broughton and the Naismith-Jones tragedies I realised what wide consequential effects the war had on the behaviour pattern of humanity, even far removed from the actual battlefield.

I was fortunate to enrol a number of elderly well-known business men into what I formed and called the Parklands Special Police Section. They were always there to support and assist me when required, a dedicated group of men who had also seen service in the First World War.

Although the area was relatively quiet in comparison to the rest of the Nairobi area, I was again exhausted and my wife also showed signs of stress.

I now commenced agitating for a transfer away from Nairobi, which led to a confrontation with a young officer who had arrived from Sandhurst complete with rank automatically awarded him, the custom at that time. I now demanded a transfer from Nairobi or my release from the Kenya Police. The Commissioner of Police, a well respected man, called me to his office where we had a long discussion. I appreciated his predicament. This calmed and satisfied me

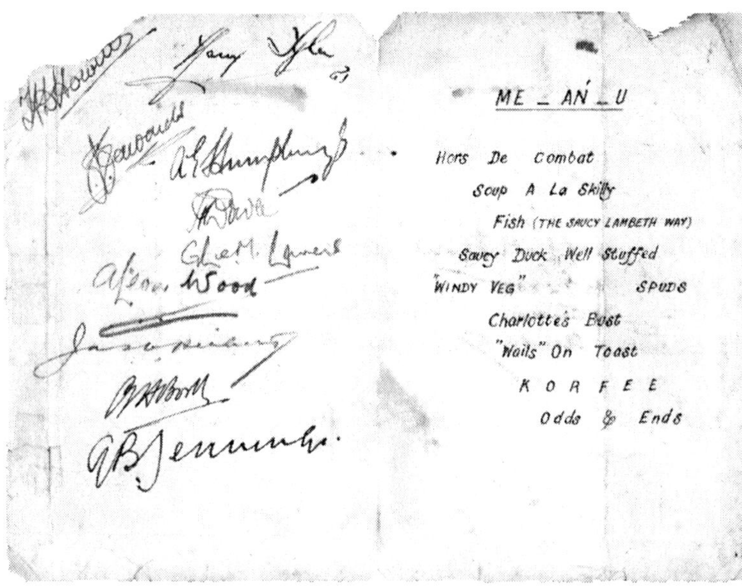

Document F *Norfolk Hotel Menu, 1941.*

somewhat, but he also realised that I could no longer remain in this province and offered me a transfer to Solai in the Rift Valley Province.

This was to materialise in October 1941. My wife was also now expecting and my mother came to Parklands to assist us to pack and move with us to Solai and further assist my wife there.

When the Special Police Section heard of my transfer they quietly arranged a special dinner for me at the Norfolk Hotel. Another of those wonderful and kind gestures from a crowd of people I shall never forget. I have fortunately managed to retain the special menu, now over fifty years old (see Document F).

I wish here to salute the Salvation Army, who became well known to me in Nairobi. They established a deep insight of the real meaning of religion in me.

These men and women of the Street Army I am sure will always receive the blessing and respect of all well meaning people who come into contact with them. *March on Christian soldiers.*

CHAPTER XIII

Solai, under command of the Rift Valley Province, was in complete contrast to the Nairobi area and was composed almost entirely of a farming community with the Samburu Reserve on the northern border. A number of farms were situated on the border and farmed mostly by women whose husbands were in the armed forces. Amongst others were a Mrs Rutherford, an extremely friendly old lady, and the Edmundsons. Henrietta the daughter was married to a Mr Horrocks, a member of the famous British linen company. This marriage unfortunately failed. Later on she married Bruce MacKenzie a member of the Kenya Legislative Assembly who also farmed in the area. He was also later sadly killed in an air crash. We got to know Henrietta very well when she later often attended parties at our home in Nakuru when I was stationed there. She was a very friendly and civilised person, an excellent friend.

This district was divided by a hill called the Subukia Hill. The district was very fertile in both the valleys divided by the hill and named the Subukia and Solai Valleys and well known for the fruit it produced with many orchards producing mainly citrus. I remember the Ireland Brothers. Barton Ireland became a good friend of ours. His wife was related to some aristocratic family but was always friendly and hospitable. We always enjoyed the company of this family. Barton was one of the largest citrus farmers who produced a delicious type of orange and also a high quality orange wine for which he enjoyed a high demand. He charged one shilling a bottle, unimaginable with the value of money today.

Barton was a prosperous and very progressive farmer. Other farmers in the wetter areas cultivated lucerne and others were cattle breeders, producing high grade pedigree cattle. I well remember one of them who maintained a small Jersey herd well known throughout Kenya. There were also a number of Friesian breeders.

Some of these cattle breeders featured prominently with their various animals at the Nakuru Royal Agricultural Shows. We were very happy to be away from the blackouts, aircraft, streets rowdy with large numbers of motor vehicles, sirens and all that went with Nairobi in those days. Solai was a comfortable and enjoyable area where the air was also much cleaner.

Solai resorted under the command of a Mr Jimmy Sweeney. My parents knew him and his wife Madge who I think also had some relations in Kitale. These were friendly people, a vast change from the Nairobi topper echelon, and Jimmy and I got on very well.

The well wooded Subukia Hill was home to a large variety of birds, loeries, parakeets, finches of all colours and shapes and also honey birds. The area did not allow any hunting, which also contributed to the quiet and our enjoyment of this area.

During the evenings and when my duties allowed I continued with my law studies applying my mind particularly to the Criminal Procedure Code Indian Evidence Act Local Ordinances and decided cases (as many as I could acquire) of not only the Kenya Supreme Court, but also those of the Supreme Courts in the United Kingdom. I still received the police magazine which was also very useful. As already previously mentioned, it was quite early in my life that I became certain that law and the maintenance thereof was what would keep civilisation going.

As the time approached for our first child to be born, I remained as close to my wife as I possibly could. My superiors were most sympathetic and put my wife in the care of efficient doctors at Nakuru where I regularly took her to Dr Ternant, a dour Scotsman who had already been in practice for many years and was always available when required. On 27 May 1942 my daughter Anne was born in the Nakuru War Memorial Hospital where I took my wife on the previous evening. This was an excellent hospital with impeccable nursing staff. I often wonder these days when you listen to the news and reports and also my own recent experience where have all those wonderful nurses gone. They were always at your side with a smile when circumstances demanded.

The matrons also did their rounds frequently, always twice a day in the mornings and again at night. The friendly approach and care of these friendly ladies, I am certain played their part in the recovery of their patients.

All went well and my wife and little Anne came home to Solai. I was all a-dither and tense. In those days attention and care to babies consisted of advice from mothers and of course grandmothers if still alive. Very few books were available. Unfortunately Anne was a rather restless baby and kept us awake almost all night, every night, until it was ascertained that she was not receiving sufficient milk. This was rectified and she became more restful.

Not long after this, Superintendent Sweeney came out to Solai and told me that they were considering me for transfer to Nakuru as public prosecutor in charge of the Rift Valley Province which was at that time in the hands of Tosh Ebblewhite, a person very well versed in law. After a long discussion, Jim Sweeney convinced me that with my qualifications and service record I would easily cope with this position. They were also aware of my interest in law.

The court was presided over by a Resident Magistrate who also enjoyed jurisdiction over all the areas within the Province. As we had come to know Solai which afforded me at least some more relaxed periods than I had experienced until I was transferred there from Nairobi and would also have to take leave of a number of new and well liked friends, I was not too enthusiastic about this move.

Long leave had been suspended because of the war and although quite young my Nairobi experiences had also somewhat exhausted me. Although Jim Sweeney was quite sympathetic I knew there was nothing either of us could do about this matter and I eventually became reconciled with the transfer and after handing over at Solai we moved to Nakuru.

I think the fact that I had been to school there and knew the town reasonably well also helped to motivate a more relaxed acceptance of this new move.

CHAPTER XIV

Tosh Ebblewhite stayed for two weeks or more to hand over and acquaint me with the circumstances which this new position demanded and also to finalise some of the cases on trial in which he was involved. His attitude was friendly and meticulous and certainly assisted me very much to settle down much sooner than I had anticipated.

Our new home was large and comfortable and was also just across the road from the magistrate's court and other provincial offices. The set-up here, although more onerous and exacting, was much more satisfactory for both of us to begin with, but was not maintained as time progressed.

One of the problems that arose was that I was without a motor car. I had sold my car to a young doctor who had arrived in Nakuru and as there were no new cars available and hardly ever any second-hand ones on the market, I was requested by the controller of transport to sell my vehicle to this doctor. I was not very happy about this, but I appreciated the situation and at least I received a fairly reasonable price. I also received a letter from the controller confirming that he had placed my name on the priority list for a new vehicle when they became available from imports at the end of the war. We settled down and my wife planted a small garden which kept her busy.

The Resident Magistrate there at the time was also awaiting transfer, I think to Kisumu, and was to be replaced by a Mr Warren Wright, a retired Uganda judge who had been recalled for duty because of the shortage of qualified people in the law courts of Kenya at that time. Again our path crossed that of a friendly couple. They were childless and I suppose because of that, Mrs Wright appreciated my wife assisting in showing her around town. My wife also enjoyed her company. He was an Irishman out and out, a brilliant legal man with a very wide knowledge of all the laws that applied to the colonies and especially Kenya.

I had no difficulty in handling any cases as far as attorneys or solicitors were concerned, but one person who gave me quite a difficult time, but also a very useful man as far as my knowledge of law was concerned, was a West Indian gentleman who had qualified as a barrister in London. He was Alfred James (Jimmy) Burke KC. Jimmy was a brilliant man and also a man of high integrity and always fair and we eventually became close friends. His neatness, behaviour and dress, always in full regalia (gown and wig) gave considerable dignity to the magistrate's court. He was known and well respected by everybody who came into contact with him. I also mentioned him earlier when I recorded the Delves Broughton case.

Although he retained his residence and main office in Nairobi, he also opened an office in the Main Street in Nakuru where another West Indian advocate joined him. Burke's business grew to an extent where he had to confine himself only to the very serious matters which came his way and very often had to turn briefs away. At no time did I ever hear or notice that he had neglected to give his full attention and time to any case in which he was involved. He never took any short cuts.

All the more serious crimes and especially felonious cases were referred to the Resident Magistrate's Court in Nakuru where his powers were comparable to Regional Court Magistrates in South Africa when we came here.

As my workload increased, my time for relaxation decreased. When trials ended sometimes late in the evening I had to go home with cases due for hearing on the following morning to prepare them for proper prosecution.

The war was again escalating, with heavy fighting in the Central Pacific, Singapore, Okinawa and Solomon Islands where a large number of young British and American men lost their lives. Young men who had hardly left school having to face the cruelty of the Japanese armies and also their air forces. Their bombers hit those congested parts where the civilian population were also very badly exposed to those attacks, involving enormous pain and suffering to hundreds of thousands of innocent women and children incinerated from the air.

The situation in Africa was also deteriorating with the surrender of Tobruk to the Axis forces. Among the thousands of South Africans taken were also some of the soldiers we came to know earlier in the war when they were invited to and entertained at our home.

This immense cruelty began to awaken some deep and serious problems and doubts in my mind and as my thoughts began wandering back over history, I began to wonder why religion in its various forms invariably featured prominently in influencing entire nations into the hatred and destruction of millions of humans not only of other nations, but also of their own. How could I possibly reconcile this with the Ten Commandments and the one so deeply impressed upon me in my own home, 'Love your neighbour as yourself'. Not to mention 'Thou shalt not kill'. After immense meditation, I managed to blank these thoughts out of my mind and continued in my humble way to walk along the path I considered correct.

Something that I have always regretted about this period is that I must have very often neglected my wife and child – a lovely bonny daughter who had also now started to walk and talk. I fortunately managed to get them away to my parents on the farm where they would at least be away from all this harassment that I was subjected to at the time.

Rumours also now began circulating that I was to be transferred back to the active police force. These rumours no doubt resulted from my remarks very often made to my superiors that I had done my share in the courts and looked forward to being transferred to a rural country district. One of the rumours was that I was to be transferred to Gilgil. A colleague of mine who heard about this told me that Gilgil was under the command of Superintendent Eddy Bristow and that he was an impossible person to get on with. This rather surprised me as I had already met Eddy Bristow in court and found him a friendly and approachable person. I however also heard shortly after this that Gilgil police station was in a bad state as far as the administration was concerned – in fact it was a real mess. I could not obtain any confirmation of this move from my superiors when I accosted them.

In the meantime I continued at Nakuru, situated at the Menengai crater which was also still slightly active. At the time Nakuru was no longer as I knew it in my school days. Military forces were stationed there and also a wing of the South African Air Force were also there with their base to the north of the town.

The conditions created by the crater and the lake below apparently caused a large number of air pockets being formed in the area which made flying especially at night difficult and at times dangerous. This especially affected aircraft coming in to land, or on take-off. An aircraft was involved in a very nasty accident when it crash landed and caught fire, incinerating the entire crew which I think consisted of three members. This also no doubt added to my psychological stress and I made it

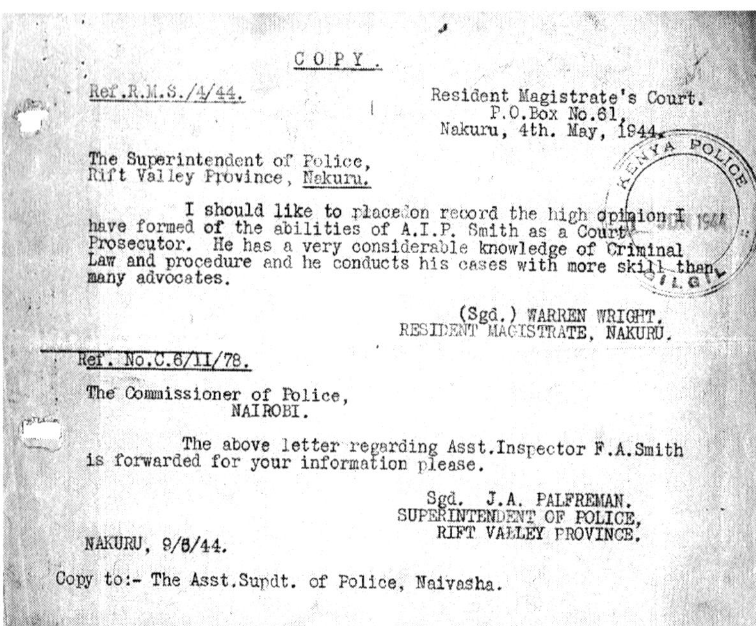

COPY.

Ref.R.M.S./4/44.

Resident Magistrate's Court.
P.O.Box No.61,
Nakuru, 4th. May, 1944.

The Superintendent of Police,
Rift Valley Province, Nakuru.

I should like to place on record the high opinion I have formed of the abilities of A.I.P. Smith as a Court Prosecutor. He has a very considerable knowledge of Criminal Law and procedure and he conducts his cases with more skill than many advocates.

(Sgd.) WARREN WRIGHT.
RESIDENT MAGISTRATE, NAKURU.

Ref. No.C.6/II/78.

The Commissioner of Police,
NAIROBI.

The above letter regarding Asst.Inspector F.A.Smith is forwarded for your information please.

Sgd. J.A. PALFREMAN.
SUPERINTENDENT OF POLICE,
RIFT VALLEY PROVINCE.

NAKURU, 9/5/44.

Copy to:- The Asst.Supdt. of Police, Naivasha.

Document G *Copy of letter from Police Superintendent, Naivasha.*

very clear to my superiors that I was not prepared to carry on very much longer and the time had now come for me to move. I was adamant about this.

When Mr Warren Wright heard about this, he called me into his office and made me an offer which really astounded me. As already mentioned they were childless and after sitting down he told me that they would be delighted to assist me to go to London to study at the Inns to qualify so that I could be called to the British Bar. I have a copy of a letter written by him to the Superintendent at Nakuru in which he expressed a very high opinion of my legal knowledge and ability (see Document G).

Although this offer was a wonderful opportunity and which I would really have enjoyed I could not morally accept it. I was married with a wife and child to provide for. One can only imagine the enormous costs which he would have been involved in, in keeping me and my family in London and to which I would not have been able to contribute. He eventually even went so far as to tell me that after qualifying and starting to practise back in Kenya, I could repay him over time or if he and his wife were no longer alive, he nominated some charity to which I could contribute the money. I was overwhelmed by this more than generous offer and although I was confident that I would have no difficulty in succeeding within the shortest permissible period, I finally told him that I could not accept it.

Another problem that confronted us was that having lost my car, it was impossible to at least get away for weekends when I could do so. Fortunately a very good friend of ours, Mr Scotty Osborne who owned some large saw mills on the wooded hills at Elburgun and Rongai near Nakuru, offered to convey us to wherever we wished to go.

During a visit to my doctor he advised me that it was absolutely necessary for me to take a few weeks' rest and handed me a letter to this effect.

I then applied for fourteen days' leave which was promptly granted and Scotty took us to my father's farm, where we enjoyed a most relaxed and pleasant two weeks.

CHAPTER XV

On our return to Nakuru I was told that I would indeed be transferred to Gilgil, which I already knew was a large and difficult district to run. It included the Delves Broughton–Muthaiga crowd, who as already mentioned owned a property in Wanjohi, or the Happy Valley area.

Gilgil also contained some very large farms owned by some wealthy aristocrats. Delamere Estates and Lady Eleanor Cole and also Mr Gilbert Colvile all running vast merino sheep farms on the savannah grasslands towards Nakuru. There was also a new land resettlement area which the authorities had opened up on the hills at Oljoro Orok and Olkalou and settled by a large number of farmers, on this barren land, some with very little capital. This area was towards Thompson's Falls.

I had some problems with the Masai, who had their reserve across the Mau Hills to the south of Gilgil. Here some large farms stocked with herds of merino sheep adjoined this reserve on its north side. Masai coming through a gap in the hills at night and stealing sheep was a constant burden. I was in continuous contact with the police at Narok.

One thing that I really enjoyed and was very pleased about was a brand new Chevrolet station wagon assigned to me for official duties. This vehicle was a new import from America on a special quota system controlled by the Colonial Office.

On arrival at Gilgil Eddy Bristow came along and assisted me considerably to get matters corrected and up-to-date. As previously mentioned everything in so far as it concerned the records and administrative side was in chaos. All the registers were neglected and many essential documents lost or incorrectly filed. Eddy was, as already mentioned, a most exacting officer demanding a high standard of legal procedure, neatness and discipline. I experienced no problems with him and to the contrary always found him ready to assist whenever required. He also appreciated hard work and efficiency and acknowledged what I did.

When we eventually moved to South Africa we again met them in Durban when we also lived there and enjoyed some happy days until he sadly passed away.

Shortly after my arrival in Gilgil the problems increased and I became more burdened when some large contingents of a variety of troops, South African, British and West African, all arrived at the camp, which previously consisted of only a small number of troops usually in transit. This camp was also not very far from the police station and quite close to what was then known as the African location where there were an abundance of prostitutes which added to my difficulties involving the troops, especially at night.

It did not take me long to realise that I had come from the pan into the fire, but there was compensation in being in open country and fresh air and not confined to a building day after day and further by some friendly and pleasant farmers in the area.

Not very far from the police station was a Mrs Ulyate farming there. She owned a fully grown black-maned lion which was tame and which roamed about freely in her yard with access even to her house. When I first visited this farm I had a most frightening experience when sitting on a chair next to the entrance to her lounge and, being attracted by some heavy breathing, I turned to look straight into this enormous lion's eyes. After getting to know this lady better, I eventually succeeded in having the lion removed to safe keeping.

There were also a number of shops or *dukas* as they were known, owned by Indian merchants. Most of these were quiet and law abiding citizens stocking a large variety of items which were available during the war, but of course excluding the more luxurious types of goods not readily obtainable and banned by import control. This unfortunately led to another problem that we had to contend with – the 'black market' sales of goods which had been accumulated and sold secretly by way of well arranged methods and systems very difficult to control.

I was confronted by many difficulties but also had some agreeable and memorable experiences. Amongst the interesting people I met here was a new magistrate. He came to Kenya on transfer from the Seychelles. He was a Mr de Letang, not only an efficient magistrate, but also prompt in delivering judgement after conclusion of the cases brought to court. He was a most friendly and interesting person to talk to, as was his wife. It gave my wife some pleasure talking to this family and especially Mrs de Letang who often accompanied him. She stopped over in our home where she related some incidents in the Seychelles and other interesting experiences they enjoyed elsewhere during their travels (see Figure 41). Ironically it was also at about this time that I met a general who had arrived here with some of the troops, a General Sir Francis de Guingand. General de Guingand I also got to know better later when I was stationed at Thompson's Falls and he commenced farming in that area. They were also an approachable family – no chips on their shoulders.

Here I also met a gentleman previously referred to, Mr Davo Davidson who was as far as I can remember then a member of the military police at Gilgil. I often wonder

Figure 41 *Gilgil house and office in front.*

whether he is still alive. He had a most interesting life and told me that he was born in Australia and as a youngster stowed away aboard a ship and landed in South America where he became a cowhand. From there he somehow got to Canada where he joined the Canadian Mounted Police, but I don't think he stayed there for very long and managed to get to the United States of America.

He eventually became involved with a gang of gangsters which had established themselves in America during the prohibition period when liquor was banned in I think the entire United States. Davo became one of the 'protection' leaders of one of the so called rum-running gangs, Al Capone or John Dillinger I am no longer certain which one. He was unmarried and landed in World War II in Europe and from there came to Kenya where I met him at the scene of an accident involving a military vehicle.

He always carried two Colt pistols in holsters strapped invisibly under a lumber jacket normally worn by him and could fire these pistols simultaneously and split a playing card set up edgeways at a range of about twenty yards. He was certainly not criminally orientated and I could never understand how he became involved in liquor-running.

I also had difficulties with a group of the military forces when they instigated problems with the shop owners in town and which were usually started by a well-known South African boxer. I shall not record his name which I still remember as it may cause embarrassment to him if still alive or to his family or friends.

My next transfer was to Thompson's Falls, but before going on to that chapter I wish to record what I always remember as my ghost story.

Returning home from one of the outstations late in the evening after a long day, I bathed, had dinner and went to bed. I was hardly asleep when my wife called me to the telephone and the Oljoro Orok police station advised me that they had received a report that a well-known farmer had committed suicide.

The home of this farmer was situated on the slopes of the Aberdare mountains with a steep incline up some steps from the nearest parking point to the house. It was a dark, cold and misty night. This made conveyance of the corpse very difficult. He had shot himself through the mouth with a hunting rifle. A most distressing event with a highly emotional and shocked wife hampering our task.

The body eventually in the ambulance, we left for Nakuru mortuary. The time must have by now moved to about 3 a.m. Approaching Nakuru we slowed down to negotiate a sharp bend in the road. I was on the front seat next to the driver, who suddenly stopped the vehicle and in a disturbed and trembling voice pointed to what appeared to be a fluctuating light in the grass a short distance away. Although this also looked mysterious and frightening to me I decided to leave the vehicle and after some hesitation I stepped onto the road embankment where I stopped.

The light ascended and then again returned to ground level, only to rise and descend back slowly. This pattern continued. Shivering, I approached it step by step, determined to find the cause of it, at times hesitant to continue, but I went on to eventually discover that it was caused by phosphorescent action on the carcass of a large bovine animal, helped along by the misty rain. I was very pleased that I continued and solved this because otherwise I would no doubt have become a believer in the existence of ghosts, a story prevalent in those days.

I had no difficulty in handing over at Gilgil to an efficient and capable colleague who later also replaced me at Thompson's Falls and who with his wife became good friends of ours. They have also now gone to what I hope is something better beyond the grave.

CHAPTER XVI

We arrived in Thompson's Falls somewhere towards the beginning of 1945. I was pleased to go there, but worried and stressed as my wife was expecting our second child and the war was becoming even more violent in most parts of the world. We also had friends involved there.

Our second child was born on 3 May 1945, again at the Nakuru War Memorial Hospital. This time a beautiful little son, who brought joy, not only to Betty and me but also to my parents, relations and friends.

Our joy was again short-lived and the first of many tragedies struck us when this young son developed a runny tummy and a local doctor or a man who called himself a doctor and who had arrived from somewhere in Europe examined our child and prescribed sulpha-quinidine, a new product which had just come onto the market. He had overlooked the danger warning that it was not to be taken by children under the age of twelve years, and our boy started showing signs of swelling shortly after the drug had been administered to him. This doctor laughed it off, but I called in Dr Arnell from Nakuru. She immediately diagnosed nephritis caused by the sulpha-quinidine. We rushed the child to the Nakuru War Memorial Hospital where Dr Tennant confirmed Dr Arnell's opinion. Our baby son died on 26 June 1945. A very, very sad time which left a mark on both of us even to this day.

As I look back to that time and also many times thereafter I often wonder, 'Is life only a game of roulette, bringing fortune to some and only failure upon failure to others?' One can only hope that something better and everlasting will result when the wheel finally stops. I often find difficulty in coming to terms with the philosophy that life is what you make it. What of all those millions of babies, young people, mothers, sick people, old people and lonely people, some dying of starvation, others ruthlessly tortured and maimed, all over the world and recorded since biblical times?

Eddy Bristow, who commanded the Thompson's Falls district, assisted me no end in overcoming this tragedy and helped me as usual to settle down. The settlers in the district, mainly farmers, were also friendly and co-operative. Both my wife and I enjoyed the attractive waterfalls, often walking down to the bottom of the gorge from Barrys Hotel, which looked over a magnificent view of the falls and the gorge (see Figures 38 and 39, pages 94 and 95).

Thompson's Falls had the advantage that it was more central and much nearer for us to visit both my parents and also my wife's, when the opportunity arose. As far as my parents were concerned it was also their shopping area and also where they collected their post. My father was also fortunately mobile, having acquired an Oldsmobile (see Figure 42).

The war was still raging with all the sad stories reported on the radio, and although there were now signs of Hitler's defeat the battles in the Pacific were increasing. I also remember the traitor Lord Haw-Haw broadcasting from Germany with all his distortions and emotions targeted at the Allied forces involving their families and so endeavouring to upset them psychologically. I remember sitting listening to my radio during the lunch hour when I was suddenly shocked to hear that a mysterious bomb had been dropped on Hiroshima which had almost completely annihilated the entire city and surrounding areas with considerable loss of life.

Our visits to my father's farm in the Ol'arabel Valley were always pleasant and relaxing. Development was proceeding and the production of wheat increased. As time progressed the entire area of this valley which was on our farm was planted to wheat and a small sawmill constructed in a space below the hill which was covered by a dense forest typical of the many already described. The forest consisted of a variety of exotic woods. Considerable care was taken to saw only old trees, mainly Kenya Cedar which we exported to the UK for purposes of lead pencil manufacture.

Figure 42 *Mother and myself next to father's Oldsmobile.*

My wife still has a sewing box made on the farm from one of these hardwood types found on the farm and known as M'vuli. The farming and timber business had now expanded to a state which made me look forward to the end of the war so that we could join my parents on the farm. Assistance had by now become vital to them.

The Ol'arabel river emanated from a spring in the forest where it started in some rocks and below which a small pool had been formed undisturbed by the destruction of man. The soft rippling sound of the water flowing into this crystal clear pool blended in with the songs of the birds, and Colobus monkeys in the trees, the colours of tree orchids and ferns and tiny Dik-Dik antelopes coming to drink from this pool, formed a picture which also remain one of my unforgotten memories.

Figure 43 *Mount Kilimanjaro.*

Figure 44 *Mother's garden.*

Here I later spent many hours in deep meditation when I went to live on the farm. This small area where the spring was had by then been completely fenced in and a locked gate installed to which only my father had the key.

At the end of the war in August 1945 I began looking forward to the acceptance of my resignation which I had tendered so as to help my father on the farm. I was advised that my resignation could not be accepted as I had to take charge of the Rumuruti area. Eric Haynes, who had been stationed there, had been promised early release to attend to some urgent affairs awaiting him in England; another burden, which I hoped would be the last, of the many in the Kenya Police which I again endeavoured to attend to as well as circumstances allowed.

My brother's final year at Stellenbosch was approaching and my father wished to go to South Africa to encourage him during this period. I was granted four weeks' leave to go to the farm during his absence. Mr Bristow kindly released a young assistant inspector to attend to Thompson's Falls while I was away.

My father flew from Nairobi to South Africa and I remember him describing a rather disturbing flight through an equatorial storm over Mount Kilimanjaro (see Figure 43). The exams were successful and he obtained his BA LL B degree.

The break on the farm gave me time to survey some areas for expansion when the time came. My wife Betty and daughter Anne also relaxed and enjoyed the quiet of this wide open rural area near the hills and forests.

My father stayed on at Stellenbosch until after graduation day, leaving my brother to attend to being admitted to the Bar in 1946.

I returned to Thompson's Falls and continued with my normal duties. On 20 November 1946 I obtained my release on condition that I continued to prosecute at Thompson's Falls to acquaint the incoming officer with court procedures. This was fortunately soon overcome (Document H) I forfeited my leave privileges and accepted a small gratuity and monthly payments for the accumulated leave which stretched over a long period. I have often regretted resigning from the Police and moving to the farm. Eddy Bristow had already advised me that I could expect further promotion in the not too distant future.

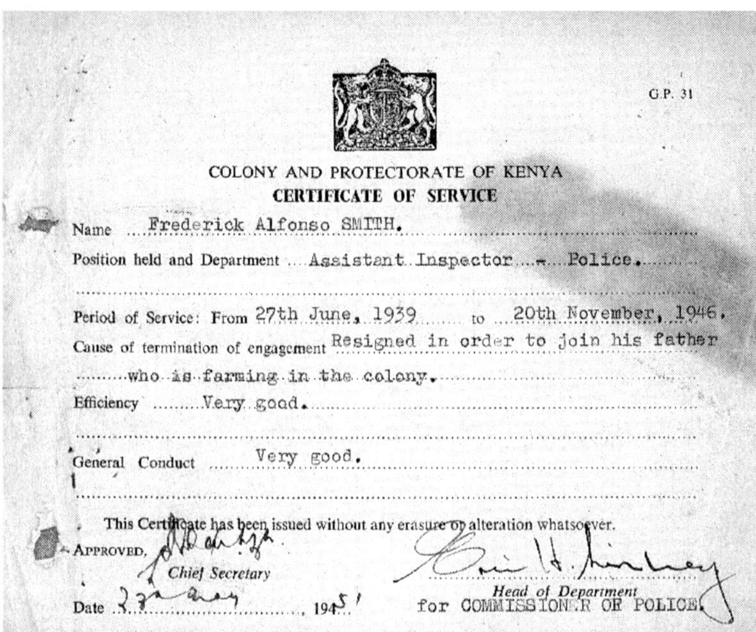
G.P. 31

COLONY AND PROTECTORATE OF KENYA

CERTIFICATE OF SERVICE

Name Frederick Alfonso SMITH.

Position held and Department Assistant Inspector - Police.

Period of Service: From 27th June, 1939 to 20th November, 1946.

Cause of termination of engagement Resigned in order to join his father who is farming in the colony.

Efficiency Very good.

General Conduct Very good.

This Certificate has been issued without any erasure or alteration whatsoever.

APPROVED,

Chief Secretary

Date 23rd May, 1945

Head of Department

for COMMISSIONER OF POLICE.

Document H *Certificate of Service.*

CHAPTER XVII

The Director of Transport honoured his promise made when I sold my car to the young doctor, and granted me a permit to purchase a new Ford which was expected to arrive in Kenya early in the New Year. I was thrilled with my new post-war car which I could pay for from savings and interest accumulated over a number of years. My wife, Anne and I drove in it on holiday to Mombasa (see Figure 45). How well I remember this happy holiday which we spent at Shanzu beach, a beautiful holiday resort on the coast south of Mombasa (see Figure 46).

Figure 45 *Kilindini Harbour, Mombasa.*

Figure 46 *Betty and Anne on Shanzu Beach, south of Mombasa.*

The resort provided separate cottages surrounding a large reception hall. All these cottages were constructed from natural materials – reeds, grass and timber found in the area. From the extended white beach the coloured coral reefs only a short distance away could be reached when the tide was out by walking through the shallow pools, where a large variety of fish and shells were in abundance.

We also visited Nyali beach, the beauty of which can only be left to human imagination.

My brother had become engaged before leaving South Africa to Tallie van Niekerk whose family has retained ownership of their farm over centuries – it is still known as Knorr Hoek – a short distance from Stellenbosch towards the hills. It was established to vineyards producing a variety of wines. Here I later saw oak barrels imported, I think from France, and stored in large cellars.

My brother's wedding date became due and he with my parents left our farm to travel to South Africa in my new car. After they left I turned my attention to further development in the areas I had previously explored. My father had sold his Oldsmobile as he was also expecting to receive a permit to purchase a new car on his return and I had to use one of the trucks.

My parents stayed on in South Africa and my brother and Tallie returned to Kenya in my car. I was extremely disappointed as one of the gears had been stripped. This was a sad moment for me demanding heavy repair costs and further inconvenience.

After my parents left for South Africa I used the gratuity which was paid to me and also what was left in my savings account to purchase a new D2 Caterpillar together with matching disc ploughs, side discs, planters and all that goes with this to accommodate fast and proper preparation of the extensions I intended making. These included the areas which were superfluous to the grazing required by the small intensive Friesian herd my father had established (see Figures 47(a) and 47(b)). I

Figures 47(a) and 47(b) *My father's Friesian cattle.*

also leased a fairly large area on an adjoining farm owned by a Mr David Icely.

The Fordson and Farmall tractors already on the farm and other equipment to which I also contributed while still in the police were put to full use. Ploughing was continued at night with the help of lights fitted to the tractors. I had also placed an order with Massey Harris in Nakuru for a self-propelled combine harvester which they expected to arrive in the New Year from I think Van Der Bijl Park or Vereeniging in South Africa where they operated an assembly plant for the company (see Figures 48 and 49).

When my father returned to Kenya and the farm, he appeared worried and somewhat critical of my large expansions and also the cost of the new equipment. This distressed me a little and I told him that he must realise that I had to look ahead and provide for the future of my family. This matter was soon reconciled with little further trouble and I went on farming while my father became involved in some other matters which interested him – farmers' associations, church matters and a number of others. He also enjoyed the pleasure of having an efficient driver at his disposal to take him wherever he wished to go.

Everything went well on the farm. The sawmill increased its capacity and income and all the wheat fields were ready for planting as soon as the rains came.

My brother and Tallie had now settled and he had set up practice in Nakuru where we later decided to spend a weekend with them. We arrived on a Saturday morning and accompanied them to the rugby ground later in the afternoon where he was to play in a match. It started drizzling and my wife decided to return to the house to fetch some more protective clothing.

On arrival there we found a Chevrolet light delivery van (as these vehicles were then known) with a canopy fitted to its rear. It carried a South African number plate with two men on the front seat. A man in bare feet and a blanket wrapped around him was already standing at the front door of the home. He appeared cold and lost. I approached him and he told me his name was Koos Meyer and asked whether this was the home of Ebby Smith. When he heard that I was his

Figure 48 *Combine harvester.*

Figure 49 *Combine harvesters in operation.*

brother and he indeed resided here, he was elated. I opened the door and let him and the two other gentlemen in. They were Mr Oliver Carey and Mr Senekal, whose first name I have also forgotten.

My wife, daughter and I returned to the rugby match where I told Tallie about her guests. She immediately recognised Koos Meyer's name and left us.

I hope Mr Meyer will not mind me recording the following incidents, but if he does or if some details are not precisely correct, I apologise.

When we arrived at the house we found Mr Meyer with his feet in a basin of warm water. He complained of severe itching and boils on his feet and especially his toes, which were very badly swollen and festering. We immediately identified his problem as jiggers – a type of flea-like insect found in dry sandy patches in Kenya. They usually attack people walking barefoot, establishing themselves under toe nails where they eat into the flesh and form small sacs in which their eggs are deposited and become hatched. Most irritating and itchy at first and if not attended to can cause quite serious infection and consequences.

The removal of the sacs was usually performed by using sharp steel sewing needles, opening the area around the sac and best done by not puncturing the outer layer of the sac.

Mr Meyer and his friends had apparently travelled over a large stretch of Kenya and adjoining territories and we enjoyed listening to his various escapades. My brother had already met him at Stellenbosch University and had related some of his pranks to us. These were now again told by the man himself.

One concerned stacking all the bicycles he could find around the university on a large heap outside one of the ladies' residences. This apparently caused considerable havoc and consternation.

He also salvaged a motor wreck from which the engine had been removed and pushed it to the main road leading to Cape Town. He eventually stopped a motorist and after some sorrowful tale about his car breaking down at a most inopportune time, he succeeded in persuading this motorist to tow him to Cape Town where he said he could have his car cheaply repaired. When he wished to return he again caught somebody who fell for his story and towed him back to Stellenbosch.

One of his acts also involved my brother who was attending an inter-varsity rugby match accompanied by one of the popular and attractive young ladies studying at Stellenbosch. Mr Meyer arrived when the opportunity was most effective, probably shortly before the match began. He was in a very dishevelled state, leading an old cart with a donkey, the cart loaded with old discarded vegetables. On noticing my brother he stopped and pointing at him he called his name and shouted in Afrikaans, 'Yes, there you sit in all your glory, father is in jail, mother is hungry and look at me trying to keep us alive.'

My brother told me he was never before or after that so embarrassed.

I understood that Mr Meyer also attached a nickname to a well-known policeman who travelled around the town on a bicycle and issued five-shilling ticket fines to students for minor offences. This old chap became well known as 'Five Bob'.

April came, wheat was planted, the rains began and continued well over the season. A bumper crop was realised, which gave me the opportunity to replenish my rather depleted resources.

My wife was again expecting a child and on 5 September 1948 a bonny little daughter was born, Marleine. She gave us nothing but happiness, joy and pleasure. She was also born at the War Memorial Hospital in Nakuru, attended to by Dr Tennant.

As time went on I could sometimes enjoy relaxing with my family and enjoy and participate in various activities that attracted my wife and children's attention (see Figure 50, probably the last taken of us together in Kenya).

The home which my father had constructed in somewhat of a hurry although comfortable for them, was not suitable for permanent residence and also too small to accommodate two families (see Figure 51). I then employed a very efficient Indian carpenter and decided to erect a large and permanent timber home with all the necessary and comfortable conveniences. A large lounge, dining-room, four bedrooms (two

Figure 50 *My wife and daughters on lawn outside our home.*

Figure 51 *First home, constructed by my father.*

Figure 52 *Our new home during construction.*

Figure 53 *Inside of our lounge.*

Figure 54 *Our home completed.*

en suite) a large kitchen and the house covered by a new corrugated iron roof (see Figures 52, 53 and 54). I also installed a 5-kW Lister diesel electric lighting plant which was coupled not only to the home, but also to the workshop. These developments I considered not only very convenient and cost-saving for servicing and attention to the various vehicles on the farm but also an enhancement to the value of the property.

The sheds were enlarged and the house fenced and an attractive garden planted. Before commencing the above improvements, I went on to improve the old home and from which I was able to establish two comfortable bedrooms with large bathrooms attached to the old sitting room and into which my wife, I and two daughters moved. My parents moved into the new house.

I continued with progressive farming, establishing proper contours where necessary on the ploughed fields and also rotating some of the older wheat lands with the establishment of *Arigrostis curvula* grass. Crops remained good and profitable, making it at least possible for me to maintain my savings to a point where I decided the time had come for me to look around for my own farm and commence providing for my children's future and also afford my wife her own independence.

My father was not too thrilled with this decision, but with the trained staff and some management already in place and established, I was satisfied that the farm could afford further advanced management if required. I heard of an excellent farm which had come onto the market and was owned by a Mr Bill Edwards. This farm was close to Thompson's Falls towards the Laikipia area to the east.

A constant river, I think the Pesi, flowed through this farm which had a waterfall suitable for the erection of a small hydroelectric plant. It was well forested with a large tract of virgin land suitable for wheat cultivation. It also had a comfortable colonial-style home.

I was interested in this proposition and with the help of Barclays Bank and the money I had accumulated, I made Bill

Figure 55 *River Pesi.*

Edwards an offer which I considered reasonable and fair. After a long discussion he eventually refused my final offer which I could not increase and I dropped the matter.

My wife and I went home and after long deliberation, and also considering New Zealand, we decided we would leave Kenya and restart our life in South Africa, to which my brother had also decided to return. We prepared the necessary applications for visas and other documents and went to Thompson's Falls on the following Monday morning. Here I walked into Mr Edwards who immediately approached me and said that he had now decided to accept my offer. I told him that I had decided otherwise and would no longer be interested in purchasing the farm.

During my arrangements to finalise my travel documents we became more acquainted with Mr Alexander Steward, or Pot as we came to call him. He was attached to the South African Consulate or Trade Mission in Nairobi. His brother

Figure 56 *Last photo of my children in Kenya.*

and father, the latter from New Zealand, had visited our farm previously with him and his wife, Madge. He also visited the farm later to say goodbye to us before being transferred to Canada. We saw them again on a few occasions after we came to South Africa and they returned to Pretoria. Again a very warm and friendly family we sadly lost our connections with.

CHAPTER XVIII

After receiving all the necessary documents for myself and my uncle who would accompany me if circumstances allowed, and after I attended to the planting of wheat and confirming that successful germination had ensued, at the beginning of June 1949 I decided to leave for South Africa. I purchased a very well maintained 1948 Chevrolet sedan from one of the Indian merchants at Thompson's Falls with which I decided to travel by road so that I could easily move around all areas which might attract me and to which I might finally move and settle. I left my family behind and travelled with my uncle Charlie Pohl as a companion and also for him to look up some of his old relations which he left behind when they moved to Kenya.

I realised that I would probably face a difficult journey as heavy rains had already begun in this part of East Africa and the weather reports were forecasting heavy rains west of the Usumbara Mountains. The roads in this area were also not very good and were in constant use by large vehicles operating between the small rural villages.

We left the farm on a Monday morning with the dew on the green lawns and the sound of the sawmills; a sad moment for me thinking that I might have to leave this beautiful country.

We arrived in Nairobi and after all the necessary documentation had been attended to and also funds transferred to Barclays Bank in Pretoria we proceeded on our way early the next morning. Fortunately the rains had not yet extended to a measure which prevented us from negotiating the swampy and muddy road areas along the foot of Mount Kilimanjaro, and we reached Iringa very late that night. The treacherous road up the mountain to this town could only accommodate one car at a time in those days and you had to await clearance, sometimes for quite a lengthy period, at either the bottom or the top of the hill before you could proceed. The hairpin bends were such that after travelling for quite a few miles, you could look down to where you started, almost within cricket ball distance.

Iringa was a pretty and attractive town with helpful and friendly people and if I remember correctly there were some beautiful flower gardens and attractive large old trees and also very interesting bougainvillaea creepers of various shades.

My next stop was at Mbeya where we stayed over to obtain permission to cross the border into Northern Rhodesia (now Zambia) at Isoka. From Mbeya I had to carry extra petrol in 4-gallon tins to Mpika which was the first stop where petrol would be available. From Isoka I had to traverse a very long stretch through a tsetse fly area where sleeping sickness was apparently occurring from time to time. This area from what I remember was almost totally uninhabited and also devoid of any wild animals. There were also certain control points where you had to drive into a chamber and the car was then sprayed with insecticide.

We reached Mpika where petrol and also tyres and other spares were fortunately stocked, but extremely expensive, when available. Here there was quite a good hotel where we stopped over for the night.

The following morning after I filled the tank and also again obtained some 4-gallon tins of petrol to carry on the next long stretch, I left Mpika for Kapiri-Mposhi and onto Broken Hill, eventually reaching Lusaka late that afternoon. I stopped over at Lusaka for a day, then on to the Zambezi River which was crossed on a cable-spanned bridge (see Figure 57) into Southern Rhodesia. We arrived at Sinoia sometime that afternoon where I booked into a comfortable hotel for a few days.

Sinoia appealed to me and appeared to be a very fertile area with well-established tobacco farmers who were progressive and also very helpful. They took me around to the farms and the drying sheds and explained the entire process relating to tobacco farming. I seriously considered this area for settle-

Figure 57 *Uncle and car on bridge.*

ment, but decided to move on and investigate other places and eventually on to my original intended destination in South Africa.

My next stop was Salisbury (now Harare) and there I stayed at Meikles Hotel. What attracted my attention and interest in Salisbury were the very wide streets in the centre of the city, which I was told had been planned by the early settlers so as to accommodate a wagon and span of oxen being turned without any difficulty.

From Salisbury I went to Enkeldoorn, a small rural town surrounded by stock farmers. This area did not appeal to me.

The rains had set in here and the roads, especially those leading off main routes, were extremely difficult and at times dangerous to negotiate. After Enkeldoorn my next break was at Louis Trichardt after crossing the Limpopo at Beit Bridge and a short stop at Messina. At Louis Trichardt we stayed at the Mountain Inn – perhaps not known by that name then (see Figure 58). From this hotel a good view of not only patches of the flat grass lands below, but also the wooded areas on the hills could be observed.

Figure 58 *Myself and car at Mountain Inn.*

I stayed here for quite a few days and met an estate agent I had corresponded with from Kenya. He was a Mr Charles Chamberlain, a real old English gentleman. He was absolutely fair and honest in all his comments on the various farms and properties on the market and which he had for sale. As we drove around I became interested in this area which attracted me more than any I had then seen. Mr Chamberlain was on in years and told me that he would also consider selling me a share in his business which in addition to the estate agency also had some sub-agencies from major companies then successfully operating in South Africa. He had no hesitation in opening all his accounts, including his bank accounts, to me.

Although the profit was not very high, I assessed the business as highly potential for expansion which this area clearly portrayed to me. Mr Chamberlain enjoyed a very good reputation in both the town and district, but his advancing years no doubt curtailed his operations.

I gave the proposition very serious consideration and often later lamented not stopping here and restarting my life in this area. It would have averted the massive costs which I incurred investigating other areas and sectors with all the problems that still awaited me and to which I shall relate later.

After calling on Mr Chamberlain and thanking him for his assistance and advising him that I would let him know what my final decision was, I left for Pietersburg.

The road was at least straight and easy, but nothing appealed to me and after looking at some farms, some on the plains and others in what the agent referred to as the Wolk mountains, I left for Pretoria, where we stayed at the Union Hotel and attended to my bank arrangements and considered the various options open to me.

My uncle also looked up some of his relations in Pretoria, and we met some more at Ladybrand in the Free State, which I also reached.

My journey ended in Zastron where I looked up some of my own distant relations. The area seemed prosperous in relation to the overall picture that seemed to prevail in many other districts. Well-preserved Chrysler 80 and Buick sedans seemed to dominate the motor car market. The Depression still appeared to concern the industries and certain other rural farming districts also seemed to be struggling. Some of the remarks directed at me criticising my Afrikaans followed by other racial comments not only disturbed me, but also raised some concern about the future.

I had by now become convinced that people of all colours who had their roots in Africa should stand together and unite and each in their own way and capacity contribute to the utilisation of the vast mineral and human resources available here to form one of the greatest countries of the 20th century.

I now decided to return to Kenya and left emigration for further serious consideration. We drove via Zambia and Monkey Bay beach in Nyasaland (Malawi) and from there through Tanganyika (Tanzania) to Kenya where I was pleased to see my family and deliver my uncle safely to his home. I was completely undecided and diverted my attention entirely to the farm and my family, while considering what I should now do. Options were again discussed but we decided as Africans we would never be happy elsewhere.

An old friend of mine, slightly older than myself, held

Figure 59 *Old Nairobi Airport.*

similar views and was also planning to investigate South Africa. We decided to fly there. News of the discovery of gold and the commencement of mining operations at Virginia and Odendaalsrus in the Orange Free State was widely reported on in the media and attracted both of us quite strongly. We flew from the newly opened Eastleigh Airport near Nairobi on what I seem to remember was the first Skymaster flight, early in March 1950 (see Figure 59).

We should have departed from Nairobi in the afternoon, but the aircraft was delayed at one of its scheduled stops from Europe due to some mechanical problems and we eventually became airborne at about 8 p.m. that evening, arriving at Palmietfontein well after midnight. After a most enjoyable meal at a café in Alberton we went to Pretoria and the Union Hotel by taxi.

My problem now was to obtain some means of conveyance – new vehicles were scarce and obtainable only on permit. South Africa was still experiencing a depressed economic period and the dealers who had any new cars demanded cash on delivery. This I could fortunately comply with and I eventually obtained a permit for a new Chevrolet (see Figure

Figure 60 *New Chevrolet.*

60) from the General Motors dealer at Louis Trichardt and we went there by train to collect it.

We returned to Pretoria with various stops along the way. Meals in the cafés and hotels were good, but the jukeboxes were rather annoying when blaring away at full volume. Coin operated vending machines dispensing cigarettes and other refreshments were also available at most cafés.

After attending to essential matters in Pretoria we went on to Odendaalsrus where I am sorry to say our high expectations were soon shattered. The centre of town and the industries were flourishing but the shanty towns depressed us. My story will later refer to an article which I wrote and was published in *Oil Progress.*

Due in large measure to our ignorance, we became involved in a field of business of which we had no knowledge, namely a general retail shop (see Figure 61), and suffered a rather heavy financial loss. This was not caused by the owners, but an outsider who made certain promises and then reneged on them. A well-known local man promised to manage the

Figure 61 *Our general retail shop.*

business until I got back or could make other arrangements. When he reneged we had to pay the owners £1000 forfeit. We returned to Kenya immediately where my brother Ebby had been involved in a serious motor accident. This news I received by way of a cable from my wife. Tallie was visiting her family in Stellenbosch at that time.

The powers that be very kindly granted me a twelve months' temporary exit permit for my vehicle and we travelled back non-stop, taking it in turns to drive. We had no mishaps and could have completed our journey from Pretoria to Nairobi in record time, but the usual immigration and Customs control points somewhat delayed us at Isoka where I was required to pay *ad valorum* import duty to the then East African Colonial Administration. This surprised me as they based this duty on the price of the car (£680) instead of the value as it stood. There were no new cars in East Africa at that time and the only value which could be accepted was the cost which I then revealed on the invoice and receipt I was carrying. I did not have such an amount on me and the authorities allowed me to proceed to Mbeya from where I could contact my bank through an agency operating there. This was promptly handled and I proceeded on my way. The amount would be returned to me only if the car was returned within the period allowed on the temporary South African export permit.

This car caused quite a stir in Kenya and when I stopped at a filling station in Delamere Avenue in Nairobi somebody came up to me and offered to buy it for what I remember was an unheard of price for any type of vehicle. This happened all the time and always caused a waste of time explaining why I had such a vehicle and why I would not sell it at any price. We returned home to worried but happy families.

The wheat had been planted and the seasonal rains which had started also looked promising. My brother had recovered and was back in practice at Nakuru.

My grandmother, now approaching her ninetieth year and still residing with my uncle and aunt, felt distressed that although I had visited her on various occasions after I had been to Zastron I had not spent any length of time to discuss Zastron and her relations still there. I felt guilty about this and I set an entire morning aside to devote to her. This I enjoyed and she was elated to hear that those of her relations who had not embarked on farming had gone into the medical field where some of them excelled. Most of them had qualified in Dublin in Ireland and a number later specialised in Vienna. She was also exalted to hear that the farm was still in the Fouche family and the homestead designed by some famous architect was still intact. What really made her proud was that one of her near relations Jim Fouche was then a minister in the Cabinet.

She remained mobile and retained her senses until she died, living with my parents in Heidelburg, Transvaal. This happened a short while after her ninety-ninth birthday which I attended and where she sat at the dining-room table for the occasion. I cannot remember her ever spending one day in any hospital. She enjoyed a comfortable home and was well cared for by my parents during a long period after returning to South Africa.

I still remained hesitant about emigrating permanently and

again experienced some very stressful times. During this period weird and ridiculous stories were reported about sightings of the Loch Ness monster in Scotland and also the Himalayan Snowman. These stories always cultivated others and the Nandi Bear story now also emerged in Kenya. This referred to some strange large furry bear-shaped animal which was said to hunt in the cold and dense hills at Timbaroa and Ainabkoi and was only visible at certain particular periods or times connected with the moon or rains. Any sightings of the animal or beast always varied in some way. Sometimes it was said to stand at a height of up to eight feet when walking on its hind legs and was very aggressive, but other stories said it was smaller and swift to disappear when seen. These stories were never confirmed.

Ironically my wife and I became bogged down and had to leave our vehicle stuck on the road about a mile from my uncle Archie's home (see Figure 62), when we went to say goodbye to them. He was then farming at Ainabkoi. It was already dark and pouring with rain. We remained in the car deciding what our next step was, but eventually we spotted a dim light in the distance and we decided to walk there. We were both fortunately wearing waterproof raincoats, a must in Kenya.

Figure 62 *Uncle Archie's home.*

This was a most difficult walk through torrential rain with muddy storm water almost knee deep at times. Holding hands, we managed to proceed. The severe lightning although frightening assisted us to avoid any injury. We arrived at this home where the door was opened by a completely mystified Italian gentleman working on the farm. After identifying ourselves they immediately assisted us to wash and dry our legs and feet and then took us to my uncle's home not far away. Again a most helpful couple.

This surprise visit was much appreciated by my uncle and aunt. A warm bath and dry clothing accompanied by a good meal soon relaxed us at a crackling log fireplace. Our chatting continued into the small hours of the morning during which my relations again strongly opposed my move to South Africa.

The 'Nandi Bear' story also brought some laughs and jokes centring on our good fortune in not being captured by this supposed animal. These stupid stories also related that this was the type of climate in which it roamed the area in search of food. We enjoyed a refreshing sleep and woke up to find that the time had already moved to nine o'clock.

The rain had now stopped except for a slight drizzle and our next task was to salvage our vehicle. This we achieved without too many problems with the help of my uncle's tractor. After the car had been thoroughly washed and tidied all round we continued to enjoy a most pleasant stay with this hospitable family for a few days, after which we returned to Thompson's Falls.

Sorting out and proper packing of our belongings then followed for transhipment via Mombasa and arranged by Mitchell Cotts and Company. The security situation was deteriorating and a number of mostly white women and children were being murdered on isolated farms.

There were also signs of yet another European power beginning to spread its wings on the northern borders of Kenya, apart from the Italians who had previously occupied certain areas before the war and had been defeated by the South African Army and Air Force.

The wheat crop was good with a high yield. The grade was of such a good quality that I exported most of the crop through the Kenya Farmers Association with some going to Baders Mills at Leslie in the Transvaal, then unknown to anybody in our family and circle of friends. Leslie will later surprisingly also enter my road.

I became even more perplexed. My daughter Anne had already been placed in the Nakuru school which she immediately took to, and to move her so shortly after she had started was worrying to both my wife and me.

CHAPTER XIX

Our last Xmas and New Year was the end of our happy days as a family in that beautiful country. A sizeable natural tree was attractively decorated and attended by my parents, relations and some friends. The children each received presents in accordance with what they seemed to desire. Our employees also each received something in addition to extra food as was our family tradition.

As the date of my departure approached I was busy attending to what remained to be completed. Moving home was, like also to many others, always an unpleasant period but this time pulling up our roots and moving not only our home but also leaving our country was overburdened with distress and sorrow. The onset of the rainy season was apparent and I decided to leave early in March.

The car boot and rear seat were packed with suitcases and whatever I intended salvaging in the way of small items, and I left taking the teenage son of a friend with me. At Nairobi I had to make final arrangements for the transfer of my bank account to Pretoria and attend to further documentation and I stayed over for the night. I also collected a letter of introduction from Barclays Bank and the manager of Texaco Oil. Here I met another passenger, a bank executive on leave from an overseas branch of this particular bank who had responded to an advertisement of mine in a local newspaper asking for a travelling companion willing to share expenses. I could only get away from Nairobi during the mid-morning and it was obvious that another difficult and muddy journey lay ahead.

We reached a district commissioner's rest camp south of Dodoma where I had fortunately crossed a wide sand gorge before it became totally flooded by heavy rains which began during the night. By morning its banks were overflowing. Although we had a short few hours' rest at this stop, I had to proceed early the following morning.

My bank friend was now rather exhausted and I think worried – I don't think he appreciated my predicament. It was still raining and the roads could only deteriorate rapidly. I have never suffered from insomnia which was a blessing and this allowed me to continue to a country motel north of the Northern Rhodesian and Southern Rhodesian border.

I regret that this part of the journey must have been rather uncomfortable for my passengers as I had to carry petrol in tins between the seats. Fortunately this position became easier and more comfortable after we reached Kapiri Mposhi where petrol was again available at some filling stations or sometimes at pumps installed at General Dealer outlets. The stopping times were still restricted and exhausting to all three of us. I was also beginning to feel the strain but only continued when I considered myself sufficiently relaxed.

As I record this story I am proud and perhaps also fortunate that over sixty-eight years of driving I have never, in spite of the large mileage covered both during the war in the Kenya Police and also during all my long journeys in Africa, been involved in any accident of any nature when I was the driver of any motor vehicle.

After clearance by the immigration and Customs authorities at Beit Bridge I moved to Pretoria where I dropped my young passenger and after parting with my other passenger in Johannesburg I went to the home of my brother's wife's uncle, Mr Hannes van Niekerk who was residing in Dunkeld West. Another family who did everything to welcome me to their home. He was an executive in some large company or corporation. Aunt Hilda was a most charming lady who was struggling to learn Afrikaans and often caused quite a laugh with incorrect translations. Uncle Hannes gave me advice on any matter I discussed with him.

From here I again travelled around and after applying for a position in the Civil Service and being turned down because my Afrikaans was not good enough, I travelled slowly through the Free State and eventually returned to meet my wife and children at Palmietfontein in April 1951 where they arrived on board a BOAC Constellation plane. The family were all grateful to be together again. We went to Parys in the Free State where we spent the first night and then onto Bloemfontein and I think stayed at the Maitland Hotel for quite a while and also went onto Stellenbosch were we met Tallie's family and relations. We had a most enjoyable two-week stay at Knorr Hoek.

From Stellenbosch we visited the Zastron area and as my youngest child was not well we decided that my family should return to Kenya. Stopping at Bloemfontein we by sheer chance picked up a newspaper, I think it was the *Friend*, where I saw an advertisement that an oil company required the services of a representative. It did not give the name of the company but only a box number. We used only Caltex or as then known there Texaco products on the farm in Kenya.

The following morning I went to a filling station nearby and the owner advised me that the box number belonged to Caltex. On phoning the personnel manager, he insisted that I send my application in writing. As my family were booked to fly from Palmietfontein within the next two days, I used my introductory letter (I carried introductory letters from Barclays Bank and the manager of Texaco in Nairobi, as previously mentioned) and was allowed to see the manager, Mr Jimmy Mackie. We had a long discussion, after which he advised me that he would consider my application and let me know during the afternoon. At the interview he called in one of his Afrikaans-speaking staff to test my knowledge of that language, which I could fortunately manage to speak well although as already stated perhaps grammatically faulty.

He phoned me at the hotel shortly before 4 p.m. and told me that my application was successful. I responded and invited him to join us and meet my wife. This he accepted but his wife could not join him as she had other engagements. We got to know Stella well later. She was a charming lady. I then took my wife and children back to Palmietfontein in time to catch her flight back to Kenya and I returned to Bloemfontein where I commenced with Caltex.

After a short training period with the local management and travelling around with sales staff, I was given a new

Chevrolet sedan and started my new career in a business totally strange to farming in Kenya. I was furthermore assigned to a very difficult and rather low oil potential rural area in the Western Free State and Kimberley district where the sales representative was leaving.

Caltex was at that time running a sales competition which was referred to as the Texpro Scottish Cup. The method for assessing it was determined by the company's head office in Cape Town; and based on previous sales and also assessment of the marketing potential in the various areas covered by sales representatives.

It stretched over a period which terminated on, as far as I remember, the end of July and was determined on the highest increase in sales of the various products in each area.

After a month in my initial area I returned to Bloemfontein and was transferred, on what I hoped for at least a more or less permanent basis, to the Eastern Free State with my headquarters at Ficksburg. Although I was again well received, I imagine because I came from Kenya, the cold weather was difficult to overcome. After staying in the hotel I purchased a small cottage from Mr Peens in Kloof Street. I also took over some furniture which included beds, a small lounge suite, dining–room table and chairs and a coal stove in the kitchen. An efficient and friendly lady servant also stayed on. I slept in the cottage when in Ficksburg but continued to take my meals in the hotel.

I was alone and applied myself fully to my duties and went out early every morning, arriving at some of the outlets before the administration staff. I also visited as many farms as possible each day. The area was mostly agricultural and prosperous with well-developed farms. Some again still in families stretching over many decades or perhaps centuries.

One of the major oil companies enjoyed a large portion of both the farm and industrial outlets and also the co-operative society's requirements. The representative became rather over-confident and by making regular and constant calls and insisting on prompt and efficient service from the Caltex depots I soon infiltrated almost the entire potential in this area. My only difficulty that arose was the shortage and slow return of 44-gallon containers.

I also managed to penetrate some of the state-controlled areas such as the railways and got to know Leribe and Masero in Basutoland.

My family arrived in about July and I remember the worried and concerned day I had at Palmietfontein where very heavy rains had at times threatened the Constellation being diverted to other airports. Persons awaiting passengers were kept advised by loudspeakers in the reception lounge. I still remember my relief when the aircraft eventually landed safely but shrouded in a massive surge of water cascading over it.

My family at last permanently united, my youngest child was carrying a favourite doll she always called Madam X and which was preserved for many years.

We stayed over at the Union Hotel and on arrival at Ficksburg the following day the hills were covered in snow which concerned and worried me.

My youngest daughter, Marleine, became sick and developed a lung infection. Fortunately an efficient and accommodating Dr Tobias soon had this problem under control. He was a brother of the famous anthropologist Dr Philip Tobias.

I was now very concerned about my family's health in this area and commenced considering moving to Southern Rhodesia. This plan was, however, short-circuited and I was selected to attend a marketing course for a month at the Houtbay Hotel to commence on 1 September 1951. The hotel had been reserved by Caltex for the entire month. This was an effective compact course, covering product knowledge and 'plus' marketing methods. A top Caltex marketing executive, Mr L. F. G. Smith, was an excellent lecturer, presenting his material by a method which was easily perceivable and understood. This period was obviously also used to assess character and personal attitudes and qualities.

The normal facilities and services as well as menu and bars were all open and paid for by Caltex. Unfortunately some of my colleagues misused these facilities especially in so far as the bar was concerned, which resulted in some being returned home.

A number of us directed our full attention to our lectures and on the rare occasions when we used any of the extra facilities we paid for them. I remember the overwhelming shock that struck me when a telegram was handed to Mr Smith during a morning lecture and which was addressed to me. I requested him to open it and if it contained any bad news to please hand it to me without revealing the contents and allow me to leave the room.

He then opened the envelope and a broad smile relieved my unbearable tension. He requested me to allow him to read it out aloud. In my confused state I immediately responded and my joy turned to embarrassed delight. The telegram came from Mr Mackie, congratulating me on winning the Texpro Scottish Cup (see Document I).

I continued to record all relevant matters in a note book which had been handed to each of us on arrival. On conclusion of the course we were subjected to a written test of which the results were only received back at our respective home bases. I remember that two of us almost achieved total success.

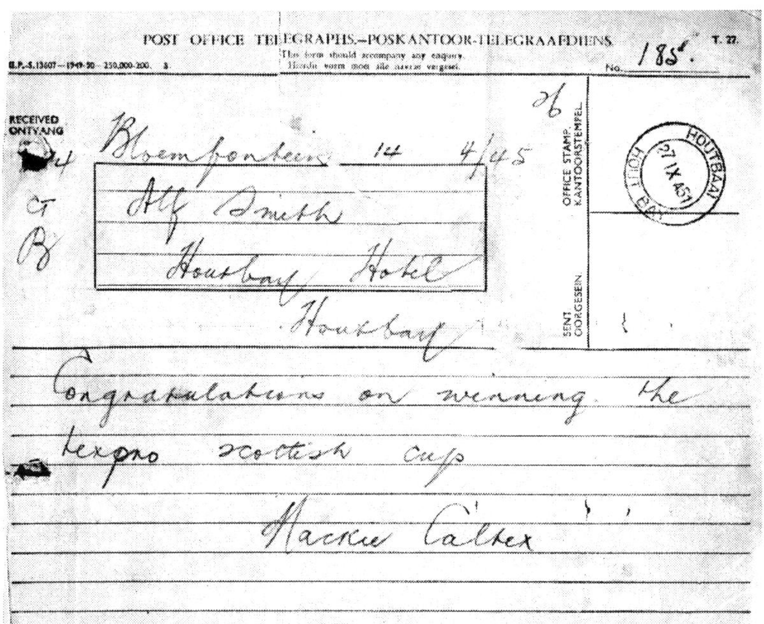
POST OFFICE TELEGRAPHS.—POSKANTOOR-TELEGRAAFDIENS T. 27.

No. 185

RECEIVED ONTVANG

Bloemfontein 14 4/45

Alf Smith

Houtbay Hotel

Houtbay

OFFICE STAMP. KANTOORSTEMPEL

HOUTBAAI 27 IX 45

SENT. OORGESEIN

Congratulations on winning the Texpro Scottish Cup

Mackie Caltex

Document I *Telegram from Mr Mackie.*

On the evening before we left, Mr Smith invited a few of us for a farewell drink and I again said farewell to a knowledgeable and perfect gentleman.

Before we left and during the course a few of us were invited to Mr Rigby's home. He was – I hope I am correct – then Managing Director of Caltex. We also attended a live Afrikaans marketing radio performance in Cape Town which if correctly remembered was called *Caltex Kaskenades.* I also forget the name of the young man who organised the event, but I know he became very popular and remained so for many years.

Some time after my return and back to my duties, I was again shocked when arriving at the hotel in Ladybrand to receive a message to phone my wife urgently at home in Ficksburg. This I did immediately and although relieved was mystified that I had to return to the Bloemfontein branch office the following day. On arrival there I was told that I was promoted to an executive marketing post in the Free State and would have to move to Bloemfontein. This was unexpected and although I was pleased to leave the extreme cold of Ficksburg it also had its problems – I had purchased a home and it would again affect my eldest daughter's schooling. At that time there was also a difficulty in finding a reasonably efficient bilingual replacement and Jimmy Mackie looked to me. This is something that has never appealed to me. I did not appreciate it. I always endeavoured to avoid recommending people to positions unless their ability in the relevant position was known to me and even more so if his position would be connected to my managerial control. I eventually approached a Mr Venter residing in Ficksburg and I think operating a small business in town. I had heard only good reports from local residents who dealt with him and his reliability and honesty also seemed above board. I then referred him to Jim Mackie and he was accepted.

CHAPTER XX

After showing Mr Venter as much as I could, I moved to Bloemfontein where I had by then purchased a home in Conroy Street in Bloemfontein North and to which my family had already been moved.

I had fortunately retained my Chevrolet car which was a great blessing. My parents advised me that they had sold our farm in Kenya and were returning to South Africa permanently. Although I advised them that I was still unsettled they purchased a smallholding near Tempe, close to the city. The name of this smallholding was Musket. It had a large and comfortable home and a strong borehole with water piped from a zinc tank to the home and garden. A comfortable set-up with a potential for extension to the already small established garden (Figure 63).

Figure 63 *Musket, our smallholding near Tempe.*

It was customary for oil company sales representatives to take their thirty-day leave break during every December to after New Year. Our first leave privilege was enjoyed at Jeffry's Bay in a small but well serviced hotel where we met a well-known cartoonist and his family, Mr Honibal. He was then doing a cartoon called Adoons for the Afrikaans magazine *Die Huisgenoot*. We occupied adjoining rooms in an annexe and enjoyed our meals at the same table. Yet again a friendly and interesting family.

We drove around and explored a large area of the coast-line visiting Plettenberg Bay and East London (Figures 64 and 65).

During our stay another interesting gentleman and his wife arrived from somewhere in the Karoo, a Mr Claasen, who joined our table and whose company we enjoyed. This holiday also helped my wife and children to become more acquainted with Afrikaans.

After my sudden promotion I experienced some criticism from certain sales representatives and junior management who had enjoyed long service and limited promotion. I can only conclude that my dedication and production results helped me to attain what I achieved. Not long after arriving in Bloemfontein I was also honoured and selected to proceed to the USA and Caltex Oil Industries there. I was keen to take this offer and the opportunity to see the United States, but because of my constant separation from my family I eventually had to decline it.

Figure 64 *Plettenberg Bay*

Figure 65 *Nahoon Beach.*

CALTEX (AFRICA) LIMITED.

PERSONAL :

BLOEMFONTEIN.
July 28, 1953.

Mr F.A. Smith,
STAFF.

Dear Mr Smith,

I attach copy of a letter received from Head Office in which they quote from a letter received from New York in connection with the article you recently produced entitled "GOLD IS WHERE YOU FIND IT".

It will be noted from the New York letter quoted that they are so pleased with your article that they would like you to elaborate on it for publication in "OIL PROGRESS".

Following on our verbal discussion, I shall be pleased if you will confirm your ability to produce a further article as now required and, in this connection, shall be pleased to offer you any assistance that is within my scope.

I would like to take this opportunity of congratulating you on your previous effort and feel sure that you will be able to produce a worthwhile article such as has been suggested by New York.

Yours truly,

Encl:
JEM/MH.

Document J *Letter from Mr Mackie.*

In July 1953 I received a letter from Mr Mackie (see Document J) in which he referred to a letter no. 716 dated 24–07–1953 signed by Mr N. A. Stott (see Document K) for L. F. G. Smith requesting that I produce an article following on a short story I had written for publication in the Caltex Magazine *Caltex Circle* and titled 'Gold is where you find it'. New York considered that the article when further researched and

HEAD OFFICE.

July 24, 1953.

SALES PROMOTION & -
PUBLIC RELATIONS.

SALES NO. 716 :

"Caltex Circle"

BLOEMFONTEIN DISTRICT OFFICE :

We have just received a complimentary letter from New York in connection with Mr F.A. Smith's article entitled "GOLD IS WHERE YOU FIND IT".

We are giving below an extract of this letter and we would be glad if you will discuss with Mr Smith the possibility of writing an article such as New York has requested. If Mr Smith feels that this is beyond his capabilities through pressure of work, etc., we would be glad if you will advise us accordingly :-

"Under cover of your Air Mail No. 990 of April 29th, we have received an excellent article by Mr F.A. Smith entitled "Gold is Where You Find It".

The article was designed for publication in "Caltex Circle", but on reading it we feel that it has so much possibility that if Mr Smith could dig out more facts and write the article at a length of 1,200-1,500 words, it would be an excellent article for publication in "Oil Progress". We feel that it could be a thrilling story of the industrial development of South Africa (with which Caltex is closely tied).

We think that what would be necessary would be largely a matter of collecting more detail - who discovered the gold, what was the immediate reaction, what displacement of farmers became necessary, who were the farmers, what acreage was involved, how were the preliminary arrangements made to develop the goldfields, what was entailed by way of building roads, bringing in machinery, hiring labour and generally getting the work of building, and developing the towns mentioned. This looks like a large scale assignment, but we feel reasonably confident that most of it could be gathered fairly easily by talking to the people who are running the mines.

If we could get such a story, together with some good professional photographs of good quality for reproduction, we should have an interesting and informative article which could have high quality public relations value."

(Sgd) N.A. Stott,
for L.F.G. SMITH.

NAS/DEF.

COPY/MH.

Document K *Letter from N. A. Stott.*

recorded by me would be suitable for publication in the larger periodic Magazine *Oil Progress*. This was attended to as requested and later published. The expanded article is reproduced in the appendix on page 169.

After moving from Conroy Street to Waverley Road where a new house was being constructed with more comfortable modifications requested by us, Betty and I decided to visit the Rhodesias on my next leave. This visit was to include the Eastern Districts around Umtali where we knew a couple whom we had previously met while on holiday at Chakas Rock Hotel, north of Durban. After arranging for the children to stay with my parents and finalising medical and travel documents we left. We found the Highlands in the Eastern Districts most attractive. We also spent some time at Marandellas and again met and spoke to a number of farmers including one of de Kock family, farming at Inyazura. We seriously considered settling here after looking at a farm which was on offer. This was also set aside after considerable discussion, in great measure again influenced by my children's future.

Figure 66 *Zimbabwe Ruins.*

Figure 67 *Zimbabwe Ruins.*

Back in Bloemfontein we again relaxed over weekends, dancing with Stella and Jim Mackie and sometimes with Gerry Brand, the Springbok full-back who later moved to Cape Town.

But I soon again became stressed sitting in an office. This became more pertinent after our visit to the Rhodesias with the large savannahs, mountains and rivers and the accommodating people we met there. We also enjoyed our visit to the Zimbabwe Ruins (see Figures 66 and 67) as well as the grave of Cecil John Rhodes on the Motopos (Figure 68).

On a later visit to Southern and Northern Rhodesia we stayed on both sides of the Victoria Falls. At Livingstone we stayed at a very comfortable resort constructed immediately across the bridge. The bungalow in which we were accommodated was on a slight incline close to the edge of the Zambezi river (Figure 69) with the sound of the Falls clearly audible. The air was also fresh and invigorating.

I took a large number of photographs on black and white

Figure 68 *Memorial to Cecil Rhodes on the Motopos.*

Figure 69 *Zambezi River.*

Figure 70 *Monument of David Livingstone.*

exposures, as also a number of 8 mm cine reels. Photographs of the monument of David Livingstone (Figure 70) and of the Falls (Figures 71, 72 and 73) and the bridge crossing the Zambezi immediately below the Falls (Figure 74). This bridge provided for the railway crossing as well as vehicles. It was on this bridge that Mr John Vorster met President Kaunda, a meeting which brought some hope of Africa arriving at a solution to bring peace and goodwill to all who have their roots on this continent.

The only problem we experienced here was from a gang of spoilt baboons which took advantage of any opportunity they saw, especially entering parked cars and causing damage and havoc.

We observed one of these animals grabbing a bottle of whisky from an unattended car. The bottle was eventually

Figure 71 *Victoria Falls.*

Figure 72 *Victoria Falls.*

Figure 73 *Victoria Falls.*

Figure 74 *Bridge over Zambezi River.*

broken and the contents lost in a scuffle for its possession. My only contribution to the welfare of this group was a packet of my children's sweets left on the dashboard cover and which was taken through a window left slightly open. My car was fortunately locked.

This tour was no doubt constructive in developing my children's knowledge and education.

THE END

Time has now advanced to the middle of April 1996 and as my future days are imponderable I have decided to record this final short chapter.

The humidity is extremely difficult to endure and fighting against man's most dreaded disease in a discomfort beyond what I am sure I have ever endured. My age also no doubt contributes to my dilemma, as also concern for my beloved wife who is carrying the full pack so bravely.

It is also now that I often wonder where from, where to, is man? From the cradle to the grave a wanderer.

Human life like in my case spanned over a period of seventy-eight years, with many sad experiences with all our beautiful children we so loved and wanted gone, whereas millions discard their children, parts of their own bodies to suffering and hunger.

Looking back over history, *Homo sapiens* is the most violent and treacherous of all living creatures – killers and destroyers of their own species – since the beginning of biblical times and even the earliest pre-biblical times.

Unless some miracle evolves to preserve what is left, this planet will once again disappear into a vacuum with nothing left. Sad; a planet unique, with all it has, and evolved over myriads of years from nothing to where it was before the industrial revolution.

It is difficult to understand that the Africa I came to know as a child has lost not only most of its incomparable variety and beauty of flora, fauna and people but also its integrity. Both black and white Africans have contributed to its development and we are now all assisting to destroy it, with no lack from foreigners who seek nothing but material gain.

Is it not for all of us to accept each other and jointly struggle to save this continent from slipping into the abyss of total destruction and eventual disappearance?

APPENDIX

GOLD IS WHERE YOU FIND IT

At a distance of 110 miles north-west of Bloemfontein erstwhile capital of the Orange Free State Republic, stands the town of Odendaalsrus, which in a short number of years has grown from an unknown, obscure country village, where the dying rumble of the ox wagon can still be heard, to a fast-developing city of world renown. This town which is the centre of the Orange Free State Gold Mining Industry, suddenly found that it had risen from obscurity to headline news after a rich gold strike in 1945.

Where eight years ago maize grew and cattle and sheep grazed, modern mine shafts surrounded by well-planned demi cities today adorn the countryside. Thirteen mines in various stages of development surround these potential cities; seven of these belong to that giant of mining enterprises, the Anglo-American Corporation. The balance are administered by five other mining groups. Of the total number of mines, two are already in production. These mines are contained in an area of about 30 miles long and 8 miles wide.

An idea of the enormous sums of money which have flowed into this once quiet, maize-producing typically rural area of South Africa, can be appreciated when it is considered that a modern mine shaft costs £12,500,000 to reach production. This, accompanied by the vast sums spent annually on salaries and welfare by subsidiary concerns and resultant commercial enterprises, contributes in no small measure to the present-day prosperity of this country. Vast Government developments such as the provision of essential power and water, the speeding up of transport by the building of new railroads and stations and by doubling of existing railway lines and the construction of roads, are also going ahead night and day.

£6,500,000 has already been spent on the provision of water and many more millions on electric power and where in 1946 Odendaalsrus had no rail communication, a new railway station has already been completed and many and frequent air services today link this area with other cities of the Union of South Africa.

In planning these future gold cities, Town Planners, Engineers and an Architect of international repute have decided to disperse centres of business and residential areas to form separate and individual cities rather than to allow development to take place haphazardly and without control. The growing city of Welkom, planned to cater for the Anglo-American Corporation, is an excellent example of this well-planned development. The advantage of starting from bare veld has been fully exploited but there are also disadvantages, the greatest of which is the insistent demand for speed to keep pace with development of the mines. In 1946 where there were only a few scattered farm houses and fewer than fifty European inhabitants, Welkom, with its present European population of 14,000 is today beginning to acquire the appearance of a vast modern city. It has a Native hospital which can accommodate over 700 patients and is the most modern in Southern Africa, having been designed on the latest ideas incorporated in hospitals in the United States of America, Great Britain and Sweden. In addition to Welkom, the nearby mother town of Odendaalsrus has also developed beyond all expectation, followed closely by the newly proclaimed towns of Allen Ridge, Van Riebeeckstad and Virginia.

So sudden has this phenomenal development been that the impact has had conflicting results on the various classes of the population; whereas industrialists and financiers were quick to realise the unlimited opportunities offered, others and especially some of the farmers in the area were left unaffected and it is not uncommon to see an old farmhouse, as it was before the advent of goldmining, standing in an area surrounded by mine shafts and other industries, calmly accommodating the limited needs of its farmer occupants. One such instance is visible from the newly constructed tar road from Welkom to Odendaalsrus where a typical farmhouse stands, as it has done for many years, without even a power connection, a few hundred yards from the enormous Welkom Electric Power Sub-station, depicting in traditional fashion the customs of a fast-dying era.

With such fast development and on so large a scale, also as may be expected, came many difficulties to those who pioneered their respective fields in the area affected by this gold strike. Amongst such, we of the Caltex Organisation also found ourselves. Bad roads, long distances and geological and climatic factors, governed by fast mining development, brought about many snags involving our transport and products and as shaft sinking developed excessive corrosion caused by highly mineralised water in large quantities, also gave many headaches. We have, however, withstood these trials and are today rapidly increasing our share of the market with promise of more to come.

Many legends surround the discovery of gold in this part of our controversial sub-continent, but facts reveal that two Scotsmen, Messrs Hind and Donaldson, were successful in recovering gold-bearing quartz from a shaft they sank on the farm 'Soet en Inval', near Odendaalsrus, on the eve of the Anglo-Boer war. These gentlemen, carrying the samples to England for analysis, were lost at sea on the turn of the last century and for many years gold in the Orange Free State was forgotten. It was not until 1934 that the first diamond drill borehole was sunk, a few yards from the spot where these two early prospectors took their samples. The correctness of their judgement is substantiated by the fact that their original shaft is situated only about two hundred yards from the present Lorraine Gold Mine, which belongs to the Union Corporation, and within the town of Allen Ridge. This borehole, although reputed to have produced evidence of rich gold, was sealed due to lack of financial support caused by the world depression which was at that time harassing the entire world. Since then rumours of untold gold deposits in the Orange Free State persistently swept South Africa, only to be pushed aside, in any case as far as the ordinary citizen was concerned, on the outbreak of hostilities in 1939. With the approach of victory, however, interest was again revealed by various financiers, culminating in extensive drilling operations and the rich strike which in 1945, brought the whole area into world prominence.

Properties in the old portion of Odendaalsrus, for which no buyers could be found ten years ago even at the most meagre prices, today change hands at figures of up to £20,000 and more, for vacant lots.

Many tearful tales are told by persons who, a few years ago were forced for economic reasons to leave this quiet village and who were forced to part with residential properties for the total consideration of the arrears in rates, amounting in some instances to only a few pounds.

Much speculation, not only in this country, but also in many overseas lands, surrounds the future of our gold industry but when American Senators of prominence in the field of Atomic Research, after recent visits, expressed satisfaction and confidence in American investments in these new goldfields, we stand convinced that with the dawn of the Atomic age and the vast quantities of uranium held in these parts of the earth, South Africa, upon whose sun-kissed shores Jan van Riebeeck landed only 300 years ago, may well become one of the most important links in western economic development and defence.

* * *

–*Oil Progress*, 1953